♠ The Education of a Poker Player ♥ INCLUDING WHERE AND HOW ONE LEARNS TO WIN ♦ by *Herbert O. Yardley*

SIMON AND SCHUSTER ♣ NEW YORK
1957

LIBRARY OF CONGRESS CATALOG CARD NUMBER: 57-12397
MANUFACTURED IN THE UNITED STATES OF AMERICA
BY AMERICAN BOOK–STRATFORD PRESS, INC., NEW YORK

Foreword

I have consistently won at poker all my life—in my home town, in Indianapolis, Washington, New York, Hollywood, London, Paris, Cairo, Rome, Hong Kong, Chungking, and on boats and trains and airplanes. And I've never lost at over three consecutive sittings.

Why? Because my method of play for each game is based on the scientific study of thousands of individual poker hands in each of all the various methods of play. I do not believe in luck—only in the immutable law of averages.

I was fascinated with the first game of poker I ever saw. It was being played in the rear of one of the seven saloons in a little Indiana frontier town where I was born in 1889. I was just sixteen—high-school class president, editor of the school paper, captain of the football team, and a fair student with a definite flair for mathematics.

I haunted the poker tables in the various saloons for a number of months, and all the while I was dealing and recording hands in my bedroom and studying them. I finally settled on Monty's Place, because it offered more color and action, and with my small inheritance and my meager savings I began to play. Aside from poker, stark drama was also being played there.

I saw the big Swede, Bones Alverson, a poor weather-beaten corn farmer, bet the last of his farm against a tent show, only to die three minutes later, his cards clutched in his hands—a winner.

I saw Jake Moses, a traveling shoe salesman, lose ten trunks of shoes. I saw a bank teller trapped with marked money he had stolen from the bank; a postmaster go to jail for shortages at the post office.

Horses, cattle, hogs, wagons, buggies, farming implements, grain, sawmills—all sold to play poker. New owners showed up at the sawmills, feed and grocery stores.

This, of course, led to frequent fights—some tragic. My own uncle, a giant of a man with a Jesse James beard, was cut down by a consumptive half his size. Uncle Bill walked a block, sat down on the corner drugstore steps, and bled to death.

I won from the first, and as my play continued I learned from Gravey Combs how to detect the many ways cheats used to fleece the unwary player. He was a good-natured country boy with huge palms and long, slender fingers. Jake Moses, the salesman who had lost his shoe samples, observing Gravey's fast deal at cards, placed him under contract and housed and fed him in his home in Indianapolis, where two card sharps taught him all the tricks of false dealing. After Gravey's preliminary education, they placed him at a round poker table with a mirror in front of his hands. When after six months' fancy dealing before the mirror he could no longer see himself cheat, they put him into big-league gambling.

The only games we played at home were deuces wild, draw, and straight draw, with an occasional game of stud. Later when I left home I learned to play seven-card stud, Hi-Lo, low ball, seven-card low, Baseball and the like. As I got farther from home I found the value of the bets smaller, the raises more frequent, and the games wilder. I fashioned my method of play after long study of each game and discovered that the smaller the stakes, the wilder the game, the easier to win.

Contents

Part One

THREE POKER STORIES

I

Five-Card Draw, Jacks or Better

———————◆———————

1.

Out of seven saloons which ran poker games, Monty's Place was the only clean one. The poker room itself was at the rear of the saloon and was about twenty feet square with two barred windows high above the ground and an iron wood stove at the end kept polished by the town idiot, called Dummy. The windows had dark, drawn curtains. The walls were unplastered brick, the woodwork painted white, and the floor scrubbed. In the center was a large round table covered with green billiard cloth and surrounded by seven cane chairs. Others, for loafers and kibitzers, were scattered here and there or were grouped around the stove when the weather was cold. The table was lighted by a single bulb, extended to the center by a cord from the ceiling and shaded against the eyes of the players. At the side of each chair was a spittoon; others were at convenient spots.

While the game was in progress, the door was barred with the usual sliding window and guarded by Runt, the bouncer, so named because of his size. Strangers were welcome after being frisked for weapons by Runt.

Monty had trouble with players looking at the discards after they were tossed face down to the player to the left of the dealer, whose chore it was to gather them up and shuffle after the show-down was over. Finally Monty put up a sign for everyone to see upon entering the poker room. It read:

Please Don't

FRIG

with the Discards

Penalty $20

Then under this sign he had impishly written,

MONTY'S CLUB

Vulgar Language Forbidden

Beneath the poster he had signed his own name with a flourish,

James Montgomery.

When I began to play poker I guessed Monty to be around thirty-five. He could have posed as Gentleman Jim Corbett in height, weight and looks, and judging from occasional fights that he got into to keep the peace, he was almost as good with his fists. Rumor had it that he had killed a man in New York who was fooling around with his wife. No one knew why he picked our town to settle in, though it was wealthy enough to satiate even a gambler's greed. He was definitely a man's man, but from the side glances he received in the streets from young girls and married women, he was not without attraction to them, though it might have been that they attached a certain glamour to him because he was a successful gambler who had killed a man.

My mother died when I was sixteen years old, and thereafter I did pretty much as I pleased. I inherited two hundred dollars from her and with this, together with the money I had saved from odd jobs, I made my first venture at poker. The take-out was twenty dollars in chips but a player could play open; that is, he could play with the twenty dollars in chips plus whatever he had in his pocket. Aside from cash in the pocket, many played open by backing their play with real property—cattle, farms, grain and the like. The player was never asked how much he played open, but if he was bet more than the chips he had in front of him, he was required to put up the difference in acceptable IOU's, and if he didn't have all the difference he played for the pot while the other players, if they wished to continue the betting, bet on the side. After a man went broke he was permitted to play one round without any money and if he won the antes he had another start.

Three games were played at Monty's—stud, draw and deuces wild. In the first the dealer anted two dollars. In draw and deuces each player anted fifty cents. Not more than seven were permitted to play, because in draw and deuces so many stayed that the game was slowed up by shuffling the discards to fill out the draw, and a slow game works against the house, which in this case took a fifty-cent cut per game.

In the Foreword I mentioned briefly how I haunted the poker tables and tried to put in practice what I had seen by dealing to myself. I had played plenty of poker for small stakes with school kids, but this was big-league stuff.

The first night I played I think my heart never left my mouth—in any case it all seemed like a bad dream the next morning. I didn't lose much, because to my way of thinking I played conservatively—but the going was rough. It is one thing to face eleven football opponents when you have ten men with you, but to face six hungry wolves alone is something else indeed.

The next few days I watched the game to get over my fear, then I tried it again. And I lost. The alternate observation and play went on until I was down to my last fifty dollars. Then I made a discovery. It all happened one night when I suddenly woke up in a sweat. I had been playing cards in my nightmare but for the moment couldn't recover the details.

I could see Monty, his face clouded in anger over some argument by the players, yelling, "Deal! Goddammit, deal!" Then he pounded his right fist on the table.

His *right* fist! That rang a bell. But what bell? Then quickly I knew. Monty was left-handed. When excited he pounded on the table with his *right* fist. Yes, I must be right. At times—it must have been because of tension—he bet with his *right* hand. Of course. When he was bluffing, he shifted his cards from the right hand to the left and bet with the right. I could see him now. When he bet he came charging like a wild buffalo. He grabbed just the right amount of chips from his stack, and *bang*!—he bet. If his opponent wasn't scared to death, he was at least confused. Monty had come at me like that every night I had played. No wonder I was afraid. I knew every move he made now. And why he made each move. Now I could see that he was dealing every time he made this fierce move at me. And every time he made this particular play he was dealing draw.

What a sucker I had been! It was too late to do anything about what was done but I might just as well go to see if they were still playing, for I couldn't sleep. I tossed in bed for an hour or so and finally put on my clothes and got my remaining cash from its hiding place and went to the back of Monty's Place. The windows were shaded but I could see a fringe of light around the drawn curtains and knew that a game was still in progress.

I pounded on the back door and was let in by Runt. When I entered the poker room the game was at full tilt, with a half dozen loafers either drunk or asleep in the chairs. By good luck there was a vacancy at the table—not exactly a vacancy, but one of the house men was playing and at the direction of Monty he was ordered to give up his seat to me—a live fish. I bought $50 in chips, leaving myself only a few dollars in cash.

When it came time for Monty to deal he took out the joker and said, "This is straight draw," which at that time meant what is now known as jacks or better. This means that the pot cannot be opened unless the opener has at least two jacks. The joker was restored to the deck if they played deuces wild.

Monty dealt skillfully, a diamond as large as his thumbnail on his little finger sparkling in the artificial light.

I had deduced Monty's trick. Someone else on whom Monty had played his trick too often opened the pot, so Monty didn't stay. On his third deal I opened for $5, the usual opening, on a pair of aces. I was sitting just to his right. He raised me $15. I stayed and drew three cards.

Monty's poker face turned into a wicked smile. He said, "I play these." I didn't help the aces. I knew what was coming but I didn't know how much he would bet. He glanced at my chips, calculating how much I had left.

Wham! His right fist hit the center of the table. He had bet $30. I pretended to hesitate, then nervously put down my hand and counted out $30, about all I had.

"I call," I said and spread my hand face up, showing two aces. Monty could not conceal a look of utter disbelief. "Well, I'll be a son-of-a-bitch," he said and threw his hand face down in the discards. "Didn't you know I stood pat?" he said in disgust. "How can you call a pat hand on two aces?"

I grinned at him. "You wiggled your ears," I said.

"Fresh kid," he grumbled. "Beats anything I ever saw."

Someone opened the window to let out the smoke. It was daylight. I ought to get some sleep before school, I thought. But the time went on. I had confidence now and was winning a bit.

It must have been after eight in the morning when a fat little drummer called Jake Moses came in. He had just got off the morning train.

"Hello, sucker," Monty greeted him. "Take a seat." Jake smiled back good-naturedly.

There was another vacant chair so I got up from Monty's side and took the other seat. It caused no comment, for players are always changing places at the least opportunity, especially when losing. I knew Monty was going to pick on the drummer and I wanted to be in a strategic position to win when he did.

Round after round passed before my opportunity came. I was sitting to Monty's left, the sucker to be fleeced to his right. "Let's play draw," said Monty and took out the joker and dealt.

I passed. The next four players passed, making five in all. The drummer, the sixth player, opened with a $5 bet. Monty came out roaring with a $15 raise. I called. Monty showed no signs of annoyance though I knew he hadn't planned for more than one player to draw against him. The drummer called, which was according to Monty's plan.

I drew one card. "Flushing, kid?" Monty said pleasantly.

I didn't answer. I never talked while playing poker except to announce my bet and the showdown. I was afraid that my voice would crack; in this case, I was sure it would if I opened my mouth.

The drummer took three cards.

Monty said, "I play these," meaning he was standing pat.

The drummer, after a peek at his cards, checked.

Without a moment's hesitation Monty bet $50—but not as boldly, I thought, as before. It was obvious to him that I had backed in the pot and was drawing to a straight or a flush. He was certainly taking me for a sucker. I had learned early never to risk money drawing one card to a straight or a flush unless there was in the pot at least five times the amount of the bet.

When Monty bet $50 I raised him $100. I didn't have a thing but I was playing it safe, I thought, with Monty betting right-handed. I felt sure he was standing pat on a bust. I wasn't concerned too much about the drummer who had checked. Even if he had helped his hand, he would hesitate to call, with me taking one card and raising.

The drummer showed his openers of two kings and folded.

Monty shook his head sadly. "You lucky little bastard," he said, and threw in his hand. "Imagine drawing one card with all that money at stake."

I tossed my hand in the discards and drew in the pot with trembling hands. I got up and cashed in. I had more than my original stake of $250.

I was shivering with excitement, and I huddled around the fire which Dummy had lighted in the early hours as if the warmth of the stove would stop the shivers. It was too late to go to school so I sat down to watch the play. I had fallen asleep when I heard Monty's fist bang the table. Here he goes again, I thought, but when I looked, I saw him using his left hand to bet. He wasn't bluffing this time, I reflected.

As the play was recaptured later, Monty had used the same tactics on the drummer he had tried on me and then later on both me and the drummer—raising and standing pat. But now the circumstances were different. Monty was betting with his left hand.

It seems that the drummer had opened with the usual bet and Monty raised with the drummer staying and drawing three cards. Monty, as before, stood pat. The drummer made aces up and checked to trap Monty, for experience told him that Monty could not have a pat hand as often as he bet.

Much to my surprise Monty bet $500 on his pat hand.

"You can't have a pat hand all the time," the drummer said, grinning.

"You son-of-a-bitch, you'll never know unless you call," Monty cried back.

"I call," said the drummer. He was about out of chips.

"With what?" asked Monty.

"Ain't my credit good?"

"Not for five hundred."

"How much?"

Monty thought a moment. Then his face broke out in a mischievous grin. "How much are those ten trunks you carry around full of shoes worth?"

"Several thousand."

"Give me a bill of sale and I'll lend you five hundred. Deliver the trunks here and I'll let you redeem them when you fork up the five hundred."

"Jesus Christ, Monty, you're tough."

"I have to be," said Monty.

The drummer scribbled out a bill of sale which Monty handed to him, and threw it in the pot. He spread his hand. "Aces up," he said.

"Well, I'll be a son-of-a-bitch!" Monty laughed. "You mean you called a pat hand on aces up?"

"You can't bluff me. You don't have a pat hand."

"No, I don't," Monty said, spreading his hand. "I only have three tens."

You could have heard a pin drop as Monty raked in the pot. He had tricked the drummer by not drawing cards.

At last the drummer gathered his wits together. He said, "Now, Monty, I can't work without those trunks and you can't use all those shoes."

"That's a fact. But you can redeem them at any time by paying me five hundred."

"I can't write a check. My wife would know if I drew out five hundred from the bank."

"Then telegraph your manufacturer. You're a sucker for cards and must have got in trouble before. It's around ten o'clock. Telegraph your people and say you need five hundred."

The drummer looked dejected but followed Monty's advice. He had the money from Indianapolis by noon, and Monty released his trunks.

Right after this play the game broke up and Monty asked me to come to his study, which was next to the card room. When he turned on the study light a dark-blue rug was revealed covering the floor. In the center of the room was a flat-topped mahogany desk, and at the end, two deep chairs and a huge sofa covered in leather faced the fireplace. One entire wall was adorned with rows of books. The others were bare except for autographed pictures of Teddy Roosevelt, Jim Corbett and Diamond Jim Brady. He did not offer to tell me how he came into possession of them and I did not ask.

He fixed drinks from a private stock and bade me sit down.

"Kid," Monty said, "that was a smart call you made last night and even a smarter raise. Now I'm not dumb enough to believe you engineered those two plays just on your own judgment. I know I did something that tipped my hand. I don't ask what it was but I'll think twice before betting you again."

I was now at ease. I said, "I told you you wiggled your ears."

"That's good enough for me. How would you like to work for me? Loggy Flick, one of my housemen, is quitting. He's cost me too much money. He plays a poor game of poker and I think he steals from me. When he's running the game he cuts every pot fifty cents, which runs into about ten dollars an hour. He can easily steal two dollars an hour from me without my knowing it. After school and up to bedtime when I'm not playing I'd want you to cut the pots. You can play at the same time you cut."

Monty paused, and when I said nothing, continued. "I'll tell you what I'll do. I'll back you up to two hundred dollars and you give me one half of what you win. I'll stand the losses if any. You keep one half of the cut. Is that fair?"

"More than fair," I said. "But I couldn't let you back me unless I knew more about the game. I'll cut the pot for twenty-five per cent of the cut and will back myself if you will give me lessons in play. When you think I am good enough to risk your money I'll accept your offer."

"It's a deal, kid," he said, shaking hands.

"Monty, I want to tell you how I knew you were bluffing," I said.

"That's your secret, kid."

"No, I want to tell you. After all, if I'm an apt student we will be partners." I paused to frame my words. "Monty, you are left-handed and ordinarily hold your cards in your right hand and bet with your left. Under stress you switch your cards to your left hand and bet with your right. That's how I knew."

"Well, I'll be a son-of-a-bitch," he said, and got as red as a beet. "And you changed seats just to get on my left so that when I raised the shoe drummer you could back in and draw one card. You'll do. You make some bad plays but I can correct that. By the way, what did you have when you drew one card?"

"The same as you—nothing. That's the reason I had to raise."

"Well, I'll be a son-of-a-bitch!"

"You said you would correct my play. Suppose we start now with the first lesson."

"Go ahead."

"Explain the trick you tried on me. Why did you select straight draw instead of deuces wild?"

"Because in deuces if you stand pat you can't make these simpletons believe you have five of a kind or a straight flush. They will think you have a straight, flush, or a full house, any one of which can be beat easily. If you draw one in deuces, though they know the four deuces and the joker are wild, they are silly enough to think you are drawing to a straight, flush, or two pair. If I raise you and draw one card you will take it for granted I have four of a kind or you might think I'm bluffing. But not these simpletons. Now, in draw, I can stand pat any time I choose and the player must decide for himself whether I'm bluffing or not. I'll ask you this—if you didn't have the edge of the right-handed betting business—I'll ask you, if you open the pot and I raise and stand pat, are you going to call me if you don't fill your hand, which prohibitive odds say you won't?"

"No—but you make that play so often."

"Sure I do. You saw Jake, the drummer. I set him up for just that play on which I won his trunks. I wanted him to think I was bluffing."

"But he might have filled his hand."

"Sure he *might* have. They all know I make that fake play by standing pat on nothing. It's like odd or even, as I'll show you in a few moments. First you have them, then you don't. Keep them guessing.

And when you think you have them beat, play the hand hard. You don't need a lock to win at poker. It's the law of averages that will win for you. I'd make the same play against a jackass who had just been beaten with a fake pat hand if I held any set of threes as I did against Jake. Set up your man with a bluff. Then knock him down with the winning hand."

As I learned later, Monty worked his bluffing trick at draw on every stranger. His unique conception of the Golden Rule, "Never give a sucker a break," paid off. He explained, "This is a club. I'm collecting initiation fees; then when I work it the second time I call it club dues."

Later, as the years went by, I worked the same trick at every club where I've played, the most recent being the National Press Club in Washington. I was so tight that members would jump to the second table when there was a vacant seat. One radio broadcaster called me Old Adhesive.

There was a house rule against looking at face cards but some of the members got so curious that they couldn't resist picking up a player's discards and looking at them. If one is bluffing, this is deadly stuff. So to protect my hand and to try Monty's trick effectively I had to wait until I controlled the discards. This happened to every dealer during the deal. Discards were collected by him so that it was easy for me to hold on to my hand after bluffing and mix it with the other cards.

We played two games at the National Press Club—draw and stud. In draw, the dealer would announce his choice: jacks or better, anything opens, any pair, aces progressive, kings regressive and the like. The stakes were $2 limit. In stud there was no ante. In draw everyone anted 25 cents and if the pot was passed the players anted again after each passed pot. To open, the limit was $1 and after the draw the player could bet $2. In passed pots the opener could bet $2 and after the draw the limit was $4.

So in a set-up like Monty's it was extremely important not to have anyone see my hand—we had no $20 penalty for looking at the discards. I worked the Monty trick only when dealing. When I decided to work it I would wait for a time when one player opened and only one stayed until my turn came. I did not want two persons drawing, for it is hard enough to convince one person not to call, but extremely dangerous to fool two. Of course, at times, someone who had originally passed backed in. Then I had two persons to fool, but that was the risk I took.

My technique was the same as Monty's. I raised the opener the limit, making sure that he was one of the crowd who seemed convinced that I was a tight player and "always had them." The opener usually stood the raise and drew cards. I would stand pat. He would check unless he filled his hand and thought he had me beat. If he failed to bet, I bet the limit, $2 on regular pots, $4 on passed pots.

I worked this trick successfully forty-one times without getting caught. And then I got careless and tried it on a new man and he called on three of a kind against my supposedly pat hand—just to keep me honest, he said.

An occasional player would complain that "Yardley is always raising," but no one caught on to the fact that I worked this trick only when I dealt. All were journalists or ex-journalists with brilliant minds and keen powers of observation. I suppose if anyone gave it a thought it was dismissed because no one would be stupid enough to work such a trick.

"Kid," said Monty, "I'm going to read you excerpts from 'The Purloined Letter.' " He took from the shelf a volume by Edgar Allan Poe. "If you give what I read some thought, you will profit in your poker playing.

"This," continued Monty, opening the book, "is one of the characters Poe invents, Monsieur C. Dupin. Dupin is discussing the intelligence of the Prefect of the French police. He says:

'Many a schoolboy is a better reasoner than he. I knew one about eight years ago whose success at guessing in the game of even and odd attracted universal admiration. This game is simple, and is played with marbles. One player holds in his hand a number of these toys, and demands of another whether that number is even or odd. If the guess is right, the guesser wins one; if wrong, he loses one.

The boy to whom I allude won all the marbles of the school. Of course he had some principle of guessing; and that lay in mere observation and admeasurement of the astuteness of his opponents. For example, an arrant simpleton is his opponent, and, holding up his closed hand, asks, "Are they even or odd?" Our schoolboy replies, odd, and loses; but upon the second trial he wins, for he then says to himself, the simpleton had them even upon the first trial, and his amount of cunning is just sufficient to make him have them odd upon the second; I will therefore guess odd;—he guesses odd, and wins.

'Now with a simpleton a degree above the first' (Monty continued reading) 'he would have reasoned thus: This fellow finds that in the first instance I guess odd, and in the second, he will propose to himself upon the first impulse, a simple variation from even to odd, as did the first simpleton; but then a second thought will suggest that this is too simple a variation, and finally he will decide upon putting it even as before. I will therefore guess even;—he guesses even, and wins. Now this mode of reasoning by the schoolboy, whom his fellows termed lucky—what, in its last analysis is it?'

"Poe is asked this question," said Monty looking up from the page. "Poe replies:

'It is merely an identification of the reasoner's intellect with that of his opponent.'

"Do you grasp what I have read in its relation to poker?" Monty asked, sipping his drink.

"I think so," I said. "If you overvalue or undervalue another's intellect you will guess wrong. If you want to know when to call and when to bluff, identify yourself with your opponent's cunning."

"Exactly," said Monty. "And that's what I failed to do with you." He smiled ruefully. "For practice you should carry a pocketful of pennies around and entice others to play odd or even. Poe calls it even or odd. If you win consistently you have proof you can judge another's acumen. How do you think our town football team won against those bruising Linton Miners last Sunday?"

"By playing odd or even?" I laughed.

"By playing odd or even. As in Poe's *The Purloined Letter,* Linton's quarterback's intelligence is just once removed from the arrant simpleton described by Dupin. For example, their quarterback lines up his team and, while giving signals, glances to the right as if looking over the defense. Next he turns his head and looks over the left defense. Then a split second later he turns his head to the right." Monty paused. "Where is the ball going?" he asked suddenly.

"It's going to the left if his last glance was to the right—that is, if his cunning is just once removed from the simpleton," I said.

"Exactly. And I flash the signal to our captain in time for the defense to meet the threat either to the left or to the right."

"You mean Linton's quarterback always looks in the wrong direction?"

"Yes. His intelligence is so low that he would not dare to look in the direction of the ball for fear our team would catch on. But there are times when he doesn't have time to go through this ritual—times when he wishes a quick play. In these cases he gives himself away by drawing back one foot or the other to get in a better position to handle the ball. If the ball is going to the right he draws his right foot back slightly, and if to the left his left foot."

"You didn't by any chance bet on this game, did you?"

Monty grinned. "I got three to one and we beat them by two touchdowns."

"Anyone else in on this?"

"Only our captain and me. The rest of the team thinks our captain is lucky in his guesses and will follow him blindly." Monty hesitated a moment. "But I'll let you in on another secret next spring during baseball season. You should win some money."

"More odd or even?" I asked.

"Yes. Linton's catcher is named Stevens and their best pitcher is called Grim. Grim usually pitches against us, as we have a fair team. I sit behind the screen directly back of the plate. Grim is a fine pitcher and has a long repertoire of pitches: slow ball, change of pace, spit ball, fast ball, knuckler. The change of pace or change-up is his best pitch.

"But let me test your acumen. Let's say the catcher calls for the following pitches in sequence—spit ball, knuckler, fast ball, change-up, slow ball. On the next batter he calls the following: fast ball, change-up, knuckler, slow ball, spit ball. Now the batter has three chances to swing. One of these pitches is known to me before it is delivered. What pitch is it?"

"Write that down, will you?" I asked.

Monty wrote the pitches in two sequences and handed the slip to me.

I studied the sequences a while. "Well," I said, "I don't know without further evidence but there is only one repetition in these two cases. The change-up is proceeded by the fast ball."

"You see, immediately after Grim delivers the fast ball, which the batter doesn't strike at no matter how good the pitch is, I signal to the coach at third base, who in turn signals to the batter. The batter sets himself for a change-up. Is it any wonder we always beat Linton when Grim pitches and Stevens catches?"

I shook my head. "You know any more odd or even tricks?"

"Well, I'm in a talkative mood and you are leaving next fall, so why not?

"Salty who plays with us is a consummate actor and a windbag but with the intelligence once removed from Dupin's simpleton. He knows what to stay on—I give him that credit. But you can detect repetitions in his actions and chatter. For example, occasionally in five-card stud when he deals and his up-card is an ace he will bet but when he resumes the deal will fail to give himself another card. Someone will invariably say, 'Salty don't need any more. He didn't deal himself the third card.' Salty pretends to be flustered with having given his hand away. But he hasn't given anything away. He's bluffing. He doesn't have aces back-to-back. He never varies this trick.

"Then he has another habit occasionally during five-card draw of holding the cards close to his face as if to keep anyone from seeing his hand. If he bets, he's bluffing. Once he heard someone say, 'Look out for Salty when he picks up his cards like that.' You see his cunning is just once removed from Dupin's simpleton."

"Go on."

"Well, there's Curley who's a pretty fair player. You can tell when he catches a card that helps him by watching his hands. He has a mild case of palsy and under excitement the tremors increase.

"Then there is Red who plays a great deal and is not too strong a player. In five-card stud watch his eyes and general demeanor. If he helps his hand his eyes will quickly follow the deal as if to say non-chalantly, I did not help. During the betting he will feel his left ear or light a cigarette or do some other thing that we don't normally do during tense moments. You can put it down in your book that the last card helped his hand and judge for yourself to what extent.

"Also there is Shorty, a weak player. If you are setting up a bluff don't do it until you have cured him of calling. Make sure that on every occasion when he calls you beat him. After about the third time you beat him he will give you credit for having the best hand. Not until then can you play odd or even with him for before you cure him he will always call.

"Bluffing should be calculated—just like a pitcher sets up the batter. You may run into a strong hand but you have that risk. In five-card draw a good risk is to raise immediately after someone opens, whether you have anything or not. Raising immediately after someone opens should be proof that you have a strong hand. Either take two cards, pretending you have three of a kind, or stand pat, preferably the latter. Bet at the first opportunity. But be sure that these weak players who always call are not in the pot or that you have taken steps to cure them.

"In stud, even with no pairs, if you hold high cards—and you have no business in the pot unless you do—you will profit by raising an open pair held by your opponent now and then. Most other players will give you credit for having a big pair and will drop their hands. Of course the player holding the small pair, since he has already bet, may go along for another card, especially if he is a weak player. But if he checks, bet, and unless his cunning is less than Dupin's simpleton he will toss in his hand. It is also axiomatic never to try to bluff a winner."

Monty poured us another drink.

"Monty," I said, "I appreciate these tips and am looking forward to further lessons, but I hope to make a name for myself in some other field than gambling."

"I hope you do. Poe did. His short stories and poems are among the greatest of modern literature."

"He must have been quite a poker player," I offered.

"No, he wasn't, I'm sorry to say," said Monty. "He was a poet and not a mathematician. He was disinherited because of his poker debts."

2.

Monty was alone in his study a day or so later when I asked him for more pointers on straight draw.

"Well, for one thing," Monty said, "you made a dumb play last night when you had kings up and were sitting to the left of the opener and didn't raise. Kings up can be beat if too many players stay. Now if there had been three or four players who stayed after the pot was opened, your hand was worth a call but not a raise, for once a sucker stays it is hard to drive him out. Strong players may fold.

"If you have jacks up, queens up, kings up or aces up and are sitting close to the opener's left, raise. If you are raised back, fold your hand or re-raise and stand pat. Of course, in the latter case, you have to bet after the draw and hope your opponent doesn't call, because his raise before the draw probably indicates your two pair are beat."

"How about two small pair?"

"Shove them. They're not worth playing unless you raise before the draw and stand pat, then bet. It's about eleven to one * you won't make a full house, prohibitive odds." Monty took a drink of straight

---

* Here and in the following sections of the book odds will be quoted such as "11 to 1." This implies that the probability of occurrence will be one in twelve. Therefore, for an even bet, the odds will be 11 to 1.

whisky. "You must remember about seventy-five per cent of all card players are simpletons. You can see that at a glance when you go into another place to play. Suppose we take straight draw as an example. Someone opens. Even a simpleton should realize the opener holds at least two jacks, but the sucker will stay on a short pair. Just count the players who stay in a pot which has been opened. In seven-handed there are about three pairs distributed among the players, possibly a four-card straight or flush and an inside straight. Four or even five players will ordinarily stay with not one of them on the average having better than two jacks.

"Why draw to an inside straight? It is about eleven to one you don't make it. A four-card flush or a four-card straight should never be played unless there is over five times as much money in the pot as the bet itself.

"Never, I say, *never* stay on a short pair. One who does should have his head examined by Doc Prittle.

"Never stay on less than two aces or two kings. If I am sitting to the left of the opener I raise on kings or aces though I never play in the same pattern. If you drive out other players and the opener draws three cards, draw three with him. If he draws two or one, draw two, and if he checks, bet, regardless of your hand. If an occasional player stays after you have raised, draw two and bet unless someone stands pat.

"If you have three of a kind above tens, don't raise. You want the other players in. If the threes are below tens, raise. You don't want too many drawing against you." Monty thought for a moment. "Oh, yes, there is one more thing about taking three cards. Your chances of drawing another pair are greatly enhanced because the cards are usually not shuffled too well and the pairs tend to stick together from the previous deal.

"Also don't be in too much of a hurry to open if you are sitting close to the dealer's left. If you have a strong hand and someone ahead of you looks like he is going to open, pass, and raise when it gets back to you. And contrariwise, if you have only aces or kings, open if you see too many players anxious to toss in their hands."

"Thanks, Monty," I said. "How about stud?"

He laughed at that. "If you get a deck of cards and deal out hands to yourself and master what I've told you, you'll have quite a chore."

That night both Monty and I played. He took care of the ante so that I was strictly on my own. Nothing much happened until after eleven when Monty was called out to the bar and I took over.

Runt admitted a quiet-spoken man of average height who introduced himself as Lolly Horne. He said he was from Indianapolis, visiting friends. He saw I was cutting the game and asked if he might take the seat Monty had vacated.

He was about thirty or so, conservatively dressed. He kept his hat on as did all of us. He wore a huge diamond stickpin which glittered in the shimmering light. But the remarkable thing about him was his hands. They were without rings—the long and slender hands of a pianist. When it came his time to deal he riffled the cards expertly and dealt in a fast rhythmic manner.

He was affable enough but there was one thing about him I didn't like. He held his cards like Gravey Combs (our local boy who was studying in Indianapolis to be a card sharp), and Gravey always told me to watch a player who wrapped his hand around the pack, the thumb, first and third fingers touching the deck.

After he dealt the third time I asked Runt to cut the pots and went out to talk to Monty. "There's a chap in there," I said, "who claims to be visiting friends. He says he's from Indianapolis. He holds the deck like Gravey. He calls himself Lolly Horne."

"Where's he sitting?"

"Next to me."

"What's he dealing?"

"Mostly stud. I told him we played deuces wild, straight draw, and stud. He took out one hundred dollars in chips and has won three pretty fair pots."

"Go on back," Monty directed. "In a few moments I'll come in and stand behind him."

I heard Monty behind my chair. I was dealing and was so nervous I exposed two cards. The stranger dealt stud the next hand. He won, getting an ace to match the one in the hole on the fifth card. The betting wasn't strong, but he must have won another hundred.

Monty tapped him on the shoulder. In a pleasant voice he said, "Monty's the name. Mind coming to my study?" He turned to me. "Kid, come along, too. Runt will check the game."

In the study Monty poured three drinks before speaking.

"Stranger here?" he asked.

"No, I came from Indianapolis to see a girl I'm going with. I went to the hotel about eleven and asked about a game. They told me about this one."

"Who's the girl?"

"That's a little personal, isn't it?"

"Yes, it is," answered Monty, his temper rising. "But goddammit I want to know something about you."

When Lolly didn't answer, Monty yelled, "Where'd you learn to deal seconds?"

"I don't know what you mean," Lolly answered innocently.

"You can tell me about it or I'll break both those beautiful goddamned hands of yours."

The stranger eyed Monty's huge fists but showed no fear. "All right," he said in an even voice, "I was dealing seconds. How did you know?"

"They make a slight swish when you pull them from the deck, as you damn well know. How much did you win? The kid says you took out one hundred dollars." He turned to me. "Bring in his chips." I brought them in and told Monty they added up to $425.

"Where'd you learn these tricks?" Monty asked.

"From my Uncle Charley. He was a magician."

"Don't you ever feel sorry for the suckers you fleece?"

"No, I don't. My method is painless. I give them the ax. You bleed them to death slowly."

"Curious philosophy for a card sharp."

"Not for a realist. You remind me of a friend I hunt ducks with. He says it's unsportsmanlike to kill ducks with a large-caliber shotgun. He uses a twenty gauge, a small bore, and kills more ducks than I do with my blunderbuss. I wonder whether it's less painful to die by his gun than mine. The ducks might give a surprising answer."

"At least the players get a square gamble here," Monty insisted.

"Between themselves they do. Not with you playing."

"Why not? I told you the game is on the level."

"With one exception. You won't play unless you think you have the best hand. I won't play unless I know I have the best hand unless I deliberately want another to win. Will you play with a weak hand?"

"Hell, no."

"Will a sucker?"

"The sucker doesn't know what a good hand is. That's the reason he's a sucker."

"Monty," said the stranger, "I heard the kid call you that—it's an old matter of debate. Something like how many angels can stand on the point of a needle. You win on superior experience and finesse; I win because I am a card manipulator. You study percentages; I deal seconds. Essentially we are no different. In the end we both bleed the sucker."

"Well," said Monty, "I'll be a son-of-a-bitch. You talk fancy for a card sharp." He shook his head. "Sure must take courage with no gun. Aren't you afraid of getting beat up or getting killed?"

"I never thought I'd get caught. I don't fool with marked cards, the switched deck, or any related card tricks. I stick to dealing seconds and have no confederates. You are the only man who has ever accused me of dealing seconds. You really didn't catch me, you know—you only caught the sound."

"Gravey told me what to listen for." Monty smiled.

"Then Gravey is a traitor to his profession. He was doubtless sworn to secrecy. It is the custom of the profession."

"But aren't you going to show us how you do it?"

"You couldn't see it except in slow motion and I have no intention of betraying secrets except to say that the trick is done by placing cards in the pack where I want them by rapid riffles, false cuts, and finally a crimp, so that when the man to my right cuts the pack, it is restored in the order I want the cards. The first card I want is on top of the deck but I deal the second card until I need the top one, then deal that to myself. Of course there are variations—but that is the principle involved."

"Jesus Christ," I said, "he must be as good as Gravey." The stranger smiled at my youthful enthusiasm.

"Keep your secrets," said Monty in disgust, "but I'm keeping that four hundred and twenty-five dollars you have in chips. It's for a private charity."

"Don't I get my take-out back? That was for one hundred dollars."

Monty gave him a cold stare.

"Okay," said the stranger, "if it's for a good cause."

"It's for two bastards and a washwoman." Monty grinned, slapping the stranger on the back. "Here, I'll show you the father—" and Monty led him to the door opening to the saloon. "See that ugly duckling getting drunk? He's admiring himself in the mirror. Well, his widowed mother owns twenty per cent of the bank here and now he's getting drunk because she won't let him marry his washwoman and her bastards. His mother sent him to Decatur for two weeks, to take the Keeley Cure. The 'cure' is an overdose of drugs that makes you throw up if you take a drink of whisky. If you can just get whisky in your stomach without vomiting, you overcome the drug. Shorty got off the train this afternoon from the sanitarium, made a beeline here and took six drinks of whisky, all of which came up. On his seventh trial, the whisky stuck, and he has been getting drunk ever since.

"Heh, Shorty," Monty yelled and waved to him.

Shorty staggered to the door of the study (he staggered drunk or sober) and propped himself against the door jamb, his ugly mouth spread in a grin displaying gold teeth.

"Shorty, meet Lolly," Monty said. "How's all the little bastards?"

Shorty didn't seem to mind, for everyone poked fun at him. He just straightened himself and asked, "You mean mine or yours?"

Monty looked startled. *"Touché,* Shorty," he said.

3. MONTY'S COMMENT: *Summary of Five-Card Draw*

The following *summary of five-card draw* will teach you how to win, whether at limit poker or table stakes:

You should study your own weaknesses as well as those of your opponents. Keep a poker face. Keep silent. Don't gripe when you lose a hand or gloat over winning one. Avoid eccentricities. Never drink while playing. If you watch yourself, your opponents, and the game itself, you will have plenty to think about. Drinking leads to carelessness in cards. You may tip your hand. Be alert. Keep your wits about you.

I'm sure you have hung around and kibitzed at poker games when all the seats were taken and remarked to yourself—this player is a winner, that one a loser. Unconsciously the winners all chatter and the losers remain silent.

I've known players who are reluctant to start playing because they are shrewd enough to know that it takes a game some time to loosen up. Some players will bet you that black is white, because of drinking, others will do the same because they do not know what it means to play tight. If you offered these same persons a bet away from the poker game, even though the odds were in their favor, they would demur. But once sit them down to cards and some of them will bet you on anything or everything. I don't know what it is that stimulates a person's desire to gamble at the card table but many players have an ungovernable urge to bet at the drop of a hat. These cannot be called weak players as against strong ones. They are pure unadulterated suckers who lose all sense of proportion. Every game has them. They will draw cards even though the odds are prohibitive against making a winning hand.

MONTY'S COMMENT *Continued*

WHAT TO STAY ON

(1) *   Two Aces or Two Kings.

(2) **   Aces Up, Kings Up, Queens Up, Jacks Up.
            (Fold Tens Up, Nines Up, Eights Up, Sevens Up, Sixes Up, Fives Up, Fours Up, Threes Up. It is about 11 to 1 you will not make a Full House after the Draw.)

(3) ***   Any Three of a Kind.

(4) ****   Any Straight, Flush or Full House.

* or **   If the pot is opened ahead of you and only one additional player stays, raise in an attempt to drive out other players and keep them from drawing against you.

***   Raise, no matter how many players stay ahead of you. If you have Three Tens or better you may wish just to call in order to entice other players to stay.

****   These are very strong hands and you may not wish to raise and drive out other players. You raise, of course, if several players stay ahead of you.

THE PLAY

I have dealt four hands as exercises.

1ST DEAL

After the Deal

1st player is dealt	J J 9 5 2	Two Jacks.
2nd " " "	5 6 7 J K	3-Card Straight.
3rd " " "	A A 9 7 6	Two Aces.
4th " " "	a bust.	
5th " " "	" "	
6th " " "	6 6 J 7 3	Two Sixes.
*7th " " "	K K A 7 4	Two Kings.

* The Dealer.

The Betting

1st player opens on Two Jacks. I would never open unless I had Two Kings or better.

2nd stays on a 3-Card Straight. This player has less acumen than Edgar Allan Poe's simpleton. It is hard to believe that players will use good money to play such hands but they do—unhappily for themselves but happily for strong players. The odds are prohibitive that the hand will not be made.

3rd player raises on Two Aces. This is according to the book. It is designed to keep others from drawing.

4th and 5th players fold because they have busts.

6th and 7th fold.

MONTY'S COMMENT *Continued*

1ST DEAL (*Continued*)

1st player says to himself he already has money in the pot and will go the rest of the way. He calls.

2nd player reasons much the same way and calls on a 3-Card Straight. A card player should learn that once the money is in the pot it isn't his any longer. His judgment should not be influenced by this. He should instead say to himself, Do the odds favor my playing regardless of the money I have already contributed?

After the Draw

1st player draws	Three to Two Jacks.	Makes J J A Q 9—Two Jacks. No change.
2nd " "	Two to 5 6 7 x x.	Makes 5 6 7 8 K—A bust.
3rd " "	Three to Two Aces.	Makes A A 5 9 10—Two Aces. No change.

The Betting

1st player did not improve Two Jacks and checks.

2nd has a bust and checks.

3rd did not improve Two Aces and checks.

Winning Hand

Two Aces, held by 3rd player.

2ND DEAL

After the Deal

1st player is dealt a bust.

2nd " " "	9 9 3 3 A	Nines Up.
3rd " " "	6 6 K 7 4	Two Sixes.
4th " " "	J J 6 6 5	Jacks Up.
5th " " "	a bust.	
6th " " " " "		
*7th " " " " "		

* The Dealer.

The Betting

1st player checks a bust.

2nd opens with Nines up. This hand is too weak to play. With Two Pair, I do not play unless I have Jacks Up.

3rd stays on Two Sixes. This is another sucker play. He knows he is beat before the draw. I suppose he *hopes* to make Three Sixes. What he doesn't know is that it is 7 to 1 he doesn't.

4th player raises on Jacks Up. This is according to my book.

5th, 6th and 7th players fold because they have busts.

Monty's Comment *Continued*

2ND DEAL (*Continued*)

1st player folds for the same reason.

2nd player stays on Nines Up. He is trapped and should not have opened in the first place.

3rd stays on Two Sixes. He reasons, incorrectly, that he still has some vague claim to the money he has already foolishly put in the pot and sends good money after bad.

After the Draw

2nd player draws	One to Nines up.	Makes 9 9 3 3 5—Nines Up. No change.
3rd " "	Three to Two Sixes.	Makes 6 6 8 7 3—No change.
4th " "	One to Jacks Up.	Makes J J 6 6 9—No change.

The Betting

2nd player checks Nines Up.

3rd checks Two Sixes.

4th bets the Jacks Up. He is encouraged to bet because 2nd and 3rd players checked.

2nd player calls with Nines Up. This is a very poor call. He knows 4th player raised and took only one card. Actually, he should never have been in the pot.

3rd player folds Two Sixes.

Winning Hand

Jacks Up, held by 4th player.

3RD DEAL

After the Deal

1st player is dealt a bust.				
2nd " " "	J J A 10 5	Two Jacks.
3rd " " "	a bust.	
4th " " "	" "	
5th " " "	5 5 4 4 A	Fives Up.
6th " " "	2 2 A 7 5	Two Deuces.
*7th " " "	3 3 3 K 10	Three Treys.

　　* The Dealer.

The Betting

1st player checks a bust.

2nd opens on Two Jacks. He is just once removed from Poe's simpleton. If many stay he is likely beat before the Draw.

3rd and 4th fold on busts.

5th player stays on Fives Up. I would not stay on such a hand with counterfeit money. You're likely beat if you don't make a Full House and it is about 11 to 1 you don't.

6th player stays on Two Deuces. You tell me what he hopes to make.

7th raises on Three Treys.

MONTY'S COMMENT *Continued*

3RD DEAL (*Continued*)

1st folds on a bust.

2nd stays on Two Jacks, throwing good money after bad.

5th stays on Fives Up. He knows he is beat and has a vague idea he shouldn't stay.

6th player with Two Deuces has his neck bowed and stays.

After the Draw

2nd player draws	Three to Two Jacks.	Makes	J J A 6 4	No change.
5th " "	One to Fives Up.	"	5 5 4 4 7	No change.
6th " "	Three to Two Deuces.	"	2 2 2 8 4	Three Deuces.
7th " "	Two to Three Treys.	"	3 3 3 7 8	No change.

The Betting

2nd, 5th and 6th players check.

7th player bets on Three Treys since the others check.

2nd and 5th fold.

6th player calls on Three Deuces. Note that he made his hand and still lost.

Winning Hand

Three Treys, held by 7th player.

4TH DEAL

After the Deal

1st player is dealt	3 3 A 10 8	—Two Treys.
2nd " " "	8 8 A 5 3	—Two Eights.
3rd " " "	a bust.	
4th " " "	6 6 J 8 7	—Two Sixes.
5th " " "	4 4 J 9 8	—Two Fours.
6th " " "	K K 7 5 3	—Two Kings.
*7th " " "	a bust.	

*The Dealer.

The Betting

1st, 2nd, 3rd, 4th and 5th players do not have Jacks or Better and cannot open.

6th opens on Two Kings.

7th player, having a bust, raises. [This is the same play Monty worked successfully so often.]

1st, 2nd, 3rd, 4th and 5th players fold.

6th stays on Two Kings.

After the Draw

6th player takes Three. Makes K K J 5 2—Two Kings. No change.

7th player stands pat on a bust.

The Betting

6th player checks.

7th, having stood pat, bets on a bust. If he has made no false move he should win. But if he has picked on a weak player to fool he may get a surprise and be called.

Winning Hand ?

II

Five-Card Stud

———◆———————————————

1.

It is said that sooner or later everyone of any note comes to the Café de la Paix in Paris to sip a drink and watch the crowd. I read somewhere that a detective, looking for a murderer from Indianapolis, Indiana, took up a position at the Café, sure that his man would show up.

Well, the detective might just as well have chosen Monty's Place. To my young mind, everyone of note came there to lose his money—itinerant trainmen, barbers, magicians, actors, jugglers, owners of shows, drummers, coal operators, land speculators, farmers, poultrymen, cattlemen, liverymen. And of course there were the usual town bastards, drug addicts, idiots, drunkards, not to mention the bankers, small businessmen, preachers, atheists and old soldiers. There was also Doc Prittle, the local sawbones, who bragged he'd taken a six-weeks' course in medicine at Prairie City and had a diploma to show for it. (I can't include the whores, because they were not admitted in Monty's Place, where men could tell a dirty story without fear of offending feminine ears.)

School let out in May when Monty sent for me. He had opened up a huge tract of virgin timber and was building roads and sawmills. He needed financing, so he said, and was going to New York to ask his mother for aid.

"How about the skinflints here?" I asked innocently. Gossip had it that Monty had played head-and-head deuces wild with Jim Baker, one of the bank's backers, and had won most of the timber land.

He avoided the question. "I sent for you to say I'll be gone a week. I'm sure you can hold your own with these simpletons so I've instructed Sandy to back you up to five hundred dollars." Sandy was his Number One barkeep. "Dummy has disappeared," continued Monty. "Get another roustabout. I'm also backing Jack Kelly with a thousand. He has more experience, so he'll be in charge." And with that he rushed away to make his train before I remembered to urge him to attend the Thaw murder trial in New York.

The week was uneventful, with no fights that Runt couldn't quell. I won a few hundred and felt pretty proud of myself. Then, the day Monty was due home, I ran into Dummy the idiot and Chic the Chicken Picker. They were at the bar, their feet on the brass rail, and about half drunk. Chic had taken five carloads of live chickens into New York for the local poultry house. So that accounts for Dummy's absence, I thought.

The idiot was the offspring of the Rand Clan. His mother was known but his sire was veiled in obscurity. No one knew whether an itinerant drummer or the girl's father or brother had sired him—the Clan practiced incest, at least, so the gossips had it.

Chic grabbed me when I came in. "Hey, kid, we saw Monty in New York. Saw him at Rector's."

"How in hell you get in there?"

"Walked in. Sold two hundred dead chickens to those goddamned

Jersey husksters and thought we'd celebrate. Knew Monty made that his headquarters."

"If Monty'd seen you he'd have thrown you out on your tail," I said.

"Don't get so fresh. Guess what. He bought us a drink."

"I don't believe it."

"Sure as hell did. You should see that redheaded whore he was with."

"That's a hell of a remark about his mother," I protested.

Chic laughed. The idiot made a funny noise in his throat.

"Mother, my ass," said Chic. "She was only twenty, if a day."

"Then that must be his actress friend," I said.

The idiot was talking some gibberish. "What's he say?" I angrily asked Chic, who could understand him.

"He says the redhead ain't no actress. She's a whore. She didn't have no clothes on around her tits."

"Monty will break your goddamned necks," I cursed at them and walked away just as Monty entered the back way.

He greeted us cheerfully and conferred with Sandy a few moments, then asked me to come back to his study. "Any trouble?" he asked.

"Nothing to bother about."

"Sandy tells me you won around four hundred. Here's half of it. Okay?"

"Gee, this goes in my college fund."

"Got financing from my mother."

"That's fine. I forgot to tell you to try to attend the Thaw murder trial."

"Being played up big in the New York papers. Reminds me of my case when I killed my wife's lover, only Thaw is pleading insanity and I pled the Unwritten Law."

"I'd sure like to become a criminal lawyer. I hope Thaw gets off."

"Well, he won't," Monty said. "There's an important difference in our cases."

"How so?"

"My wife's lover was fooling around with her *after* she was married. White did it before marriage, not after."

2.

I glanced at the clock on the wall in Monty's study. Jack Kelly and I had been working the poker room in four-hour shifts, catching a bit of sleep when the opportunity offered. I had another hour to loaf before relieving him.

I said to Monty, "I'll scribble some combinations of cards on this pad. You told me before you went to New York, you stay for the third card in stud only when you have two face cards, including the ace or ten back to back; such as:

J 10
J J
J Q
J K
J A

and those combinations reversed:

10 J
J J
Q J
K J
A J

"That's correct," Monty said, "but for one point. Suppose you hold Q J. You do not stay if your opponent holds two of these face cards exposed, either two queens, two jacks or a queen and a jack. If they hold only one of the face cards exposed, either one queen or one jack, you stay."

"But," I said, "you do fold after the third card unless the third card is a 10 or better, such as J Q 10."

"That's right," he said, "only it's more important that the high card be in the hole. If you hold" (and he took out his pencil to demonstrate) "A K and hit the ace, you have A K A. This is a lock unless one or more of your opponents have an open pair such as ? 4 4."

"You also said you play A x and K x." [x indicates any card below a 10.]

"Yes," said Monty, "but if your opponents hold either the ace or king exposed, you fold."

"Also," I said, "you fold unless the next card is a 10 or better such as A x Q. Now," I asked, "suppose you hold J Q 10 and one of your opponents holds ? 4 4 and bets on the pair? What do you do?"

"I fold, of course," he said.

"Suppose you matched your hole card J Q J on the third card and your opponent holds ? 4 4. What do you do?"

"I hold two jacks concealed, and the opponent holds two exposed fours. I can beat what I see on the board, so raise him if he bets. If he checks, I bet."

"Suppose after you raise him, he raises you back?"

"Now the plot thickens," Monty said smiling. "Caution should tell me to fold. If he's a sucker he has three fours and is too anxious to expose his holding to wait for higher stakes. If he's a strong player, look out. He may be trying a bluff to run you out, pretending he has three fours, especially if he judges you a simpleton."

"Am I?"

"You're learning," Monty said.

"Now suppose," I said, "you hold after the fourth card J Q 10 7. The fourth card is below a 10."

"I stay regardless of the size of the fourth card, with one exception. If I have only one opponent and he has a king or an ace over me I am beat in sight unless I make a pair or catch an ace. I would fold if I'm beat in sight at this point of the game; that is, if the opponent bets. If he checks, I stay, of course."

"To be repetitious," I said, "you fold holding A x x or K x x or J Q x, and stay holding A x 10 or K x 10 or J Q 10. I gather you stay if the fourth card is below a ten and you're not beat in sight such as A x 10 x."

"No, you're wrong with the last example. But I do stay on A x 10 J. I want three high cards to draw to. The only reason I draw to A x and K x is because if I hit I probably win the pot with two aces or two kings."

"But you do stay," I said, "on J Q 10 7, if no pair is showing?"

"Yes, I have three high cards to hit."

"Now suppose you hold J Q Q and your opponent holds ? A 3 and you bet the two queens and your opponent calls. How do you judge the play?"

"If the opponent is a strong player he may be sucking me in with two aces. If he's a simpleton, he's probably betting that the hand is improved on the next card."

"Well," I said, "suppose you draw the fourth card, making J Q Q 4, and your opponent draws a 10, making ? A 3 10. What do you do?"

"The answer is the same," said Monty. "If he's a simpleton I bet the two queens again. Ordinarily the simpleton won't stand two bets unless he has you beat. If he's a strong player, I get cautious and check. If the strong player bets, he usually has me beat. Of course he may be bluffing. It's a good play to make. I'd have to judge my man."

Monty was the keenest player I have ever known. He trained like an athlete and seemed almost clairvoyant at times. It may be that some movement on the part of his opponent, a tremor, a flicker of the eye, talkie-talk or what have you, even something unknown to Monty's consciousness, tipped the opponent's hand, telling Monty when to call, bet or raise. Watching him play I was tempted to believe in thought transference, and I am not sure now that he was not clairvoyant. I do not mean this in the sense that he knew the card his opponent was going to draw before it left the deck—but once the opponent *knew* the card, I often felt that Monty knew it too.

3.

That night I found seated at the table Hairlip Slocum, the banker's son; Salty, the horse trader; Chic Chillum, the chicken picker; Bert Wills, the land speculator, and Doc Prittle. Chic, Salty and Doc were small fry. Hairlip, if he could get the money from his dad, could be tapped. Bert was land poor with extensive timber and farm holdings.

Monty was cutting the game so I played extra cautiously because I had to ante. The game had been droning along for a couple of hours when suddenly it came to life. Hairlip was dealing stud and had caught an ace on the third card, making ? 7 A. Monty held two sevens exposed, ? 7 7. All other players had folded. The betting in the first round had been $5.

Monty was high with ? 7 7, and bet $10. The other players folded, except Hairlip, who raised Monty $20. Monty just called. For some reason unknown to me, Monty was betting with his right hand again. He just called the $20 raise.

I pricked up my ears, for this wasn't like Monty. If he had only two sevens, he should have folded if he was playing the book, since Hairlip's hand of ? 7 A looked like two aces. But Monty just called. Hairlip could not restrain his pleasure at the turn of events. He skinned back his hairlip, revealing beautiful white teeth.

On the fifth card Hairlip drew a 10, making ? 7 A 10, and Monty drew a five, making ? 7 7 5.

Had Hairlip listened to our previous conversation he would have known Monty had three sevens and was playing possum for the kill. Monty couldn't have two pair—sevens and fives—for even the most inveterate sucker would not draw to 5 7. And if Monty had only two sevens he would not call what looked like two aces and hope to draw out. Monty must have set up Hairlip at some previous session and was going to slip him the change-up ball, I felt sure. But why did he bet with his *right* hand, the hand he used when he was bluffing?

After the fourth card, Hairlip bet $50. Monty, hesitating a moment, just called.

On the fifth card Hairlip drew the second ten, making ? 7 A 10 10, and Monty drew the queen, making ? 7 7 5 Q.

I glanced at Monty to see if I could read his mind. The second ten that Hairlip had drawn would have been dangerous except for the fact that two tens had been folded—one by Chic and the other by Doc. This made it a dead certainty that Hairlip did not hold three tens. I was sure Monty knew this and knew also he had a lock with three sevens.

Hairlip had obviously made aces over tens. He bet $100.

Monty reached for his wallet. He threw in one $100 bill. Then three $500 bills.

"I raise you fifteen hundred dollars," he boomed.

Hairlip scratched his head for a moment and looked at Monty's cards. I thought I knew what was going on in his mind. He figured the queen, Monty's last card, had paired with Monty's hole card, making queens up. This would account for Monty's boldness in betting $1500. Had he known Monty's style of play, he would have known that his deduction was in error because Monty would never draw to Q 7. He would have folded in the first place.

"Do something, goddammit," yelled Monty. "You're delaying the game."

"I'm calling but I'm out of chips."

"Then toss in some cash."

"Christ, you know I don't carry money around like you do."

"You mean you're playing showdown?"

"Hell, no. You know I'm good for fifteen hundred dollars. I'll give you an IOU."

"You will in a pig's ass," said Monty. "I hold five hundred dollars of your lousy IOU's now."

"I'll pay you," Hairlip whined, "when I can. You know the old man is pretty tight with me."

"More to his credit. Glad to know there's something good about the old son-of-a-bitch." Monty pretended to be disgusted. "Come on, let's get down to business."

"If you won't take an IOU, what can I do?"

This was what Monty was waiting for. I knew this because he had had his eye on Hairlip's pair of matched geldings. He had told me once, "Kid, I'm going to own that rig some day."

"You can make out a bill of sale," Monty said, "for your rig, including the geldings."

Hairlip rose from his seat, his cards in his hand. "Sit down, goddammit," cried Monty, "and keep those cards on the table. You make me as nervous as a whore in church."

"All right," said Hairlip. "Get me a bill of sale."

Monty directed me to go to the bar and get a pad of sales slips, pen and ink. I could feel the pounding at my ears. Jesus, I thought, Monty has Hairlip trapped. When I returned with the slips, Hairlip filled in the blanks and paused to consider a price.

"I imported those geldings," he said, "from Indianapolis. The whole outfit including harness cost me three thousand dollars."

"You owe fifteen hundred dollars in the pot. Make the bill of sale for two thousand dollars and I'll give you the difference."

"Christ, Monty, you're skinning me out of a thousand."

"Your old man skins me out of more than that every time I come in for a loan."

"But, Monty. This is robbery."

"Are you going to call or not?" Monty said icily.

Hairlip filled in $2000 and tossed the paper in the pot. "I want five hundred dollars in change."

Monty opened his wallet again and drew out a number of slips of paper. "Here it is, your IOU for five hundred dollars," he said, and tossed Hairlip the slip of paper.

"Christ," protested Hairlip, "I want cash. Hold this a while."

"I've held it for a month now."

"You're a hard man, with ice in his veins," complained Hairlip and tore up the IOU.

"What you got?" asked Monty.

"I called you."

"So you did," Monty said, and spread his hand. "Three sevens beats aces up in my book." He raked in the pot. "Where's the geldings?"

"Hitched out in front." Hairlip tore up his cards and snarled at Monty, "You common son-of-a-bitch, you tricked me!"

"You tricked yourself, simpleton." He turned to Jack who was watching. "Take over, Jack, if anyone wants to continue." To me he said, "Check out, kid, and let's go see our new red wagon."

We found the rig at the hitch ring where Hairlip had said it was. Monty stood off admiringly, then examined the black geldings' teeth to see their age, stood back again to regard their cropped tails.

"Four-year-olds," he said. "Matched like two black peas in a pod."

"And cost you nothing." I grinned.

"Nothing!" he exclaimed. "How much money do you think I lost back East before I got some sense?"

"I hadn't thought about your ever having lost."

"Well, I did, and for higher stakes than we play here. You're lucky, kid. You're learning as you go along. I had no one to point out my mistakes. I had to learn the hard way." He seemed lost in thought.

I broke the silence by asking, "Why did you use your right hand when you bet Hairlip? For a moment you had me fooled."

Monty grinned. "Just in case Hairlip had observed my damned-fool habit of betting with my right hand when I am bluffing. But I was taking needless precautions."

"I knew from the play that you had two sevens backed up and made the third seven on the third card, so I wasn't worried too much. But do you always draw to small pairs if you have them backed up?"

"If they are eights or less I take only one card, and if I don't make threes at once, I fold. It's a sucker play to draw the limit to a small pair. If you don't help, you're licked. The betting gets too expensive. But if they are nines or better I draw the limit unless meanwhile the play indicates I am beat." Monty lifted the buggy whip from the socket at the driver's seat and climbed in the rig. "Hop in, kid, and we'll see how fast these geldings can trot."

Monty started the geldings at a fast clip, then eased them down for a breather two miles farther at the Devil's Tea Table, which actually looked like a table some thirty feet in the air, formed doubtless by the glacial age.

He walked the horses along a grove of maple trees called Lovers' Lane. The moon was shining through the leaves.

"Got a girl, kid?" he asked suddenly.

"Sure," I said.

"There's something seductive about the smell of horses, moonlight, and wet dew glistening on the green grass, isn't there?"

"Why, Monty," I said, laughing, "I didn't know you were a poet. What's the order of seduction?"

"Separately, they're not compelling. As a whole, no girl can withstand them."

"My girl isn't that kind of a girl," I said.

"Any girl is—with no reflection on her morals."

"Monty, you're a pessimist."

"Maybe I am, at that," he said. I thought there was a note of sadness in his voice.

4. MONTY'S COMMENT: *Summary of Five-Card Stud*

Winning at stud poker is simple enough, either limited poker or table stakes. The secret is to stay on higher cards than your opponents do. I play if I hold the following combinations, but if two of the cards are exposed, I fold. I stay if only one is exposed, with the exception noted below.

WHAT TO STAY ON

(1) A-A, A-K, A-Q, A-J, A-10,
    K-A, K-K, K-Q, K-J, K-10,
    Q-A, Q-K, Q-Q, Q-J, Q-10,
    J-A, J-K, J-Q, J-J, J-10,
    10-A, 10-K, 10-Q, 10-J, 10-10.

    I also stay on

MONTY'S COMMENT *Continued*

(2) A-9, A-8, A-7, A-6, A-5, A-4, A-3, A-2,
K-9, K-8, K-7, K-6, K-5, K-4, K-3, K-2.

But fold if one Ace or one King is exposed.

Under (1) and (2), the 3rd card must be above a Nine for me to draw the 4th card. If I then have 3 cards above a Nine, I will take the 4th and 5th cards unless I am beat in sight or unless I have reason to believe I am beat by a concealed pair. Of course, if I have a big pair back to back, I naturally stay, regardless of the size of the 3rd or 4th cards.

(3) I will play 9-9 backed up until I am beat in sight or until I think I am beat by a concealed pair.

(4) I will take only one card to small back-up pairs such as 2-2, 3-3, 4-4, 5-5, 6-6, 7-7, 8-8. If I make a set of Threes on the 3rd card of course I will stay. My refusal to take more than one card to these pairs is my greatest contribution to Five-Card Stud. I know you may be tempted to take more cards to a small pair, but don't do it. To do so will keep you broke. Here's why:

First, the betting gets too stiff to warrant taking more cards. The percentages are against you.

Second, in seven-handed Stud, if everyone draws cards, four will pair. And it is just as easy to make a *big* pair as it is a small one if, *when you stay,* you hold high cards. So why draw more than one to a small pair?

THE PLAY

(I have dealt three hands as exercises.)

1ST DEAL

The Deal

				One Down	One Up
1st player	is	dealt		K	A
2nd	"	"	"	6	6
3rd	"	"	"	K	7
4th	"	"	"	8	9
5th	"	"	"	3	2
6th	"	"	"	J	8
7th	"	"	"	2	A

The Betting

1st player is high with the Ace. He bets.
2nd with Two Sixes just calls.
3rd calls on K-7.
4th calls on 8-9. I would fold this hand.
5th folds on 3-2. A bust.
6th calls on J-8. I would fold this.
7th calls on 2-A. I would fold.

MONTY'S COMMENT *Continued*

1ST DEAL (*Continued*)

The Deal

			One Down	Two Up	
1st player is dealt			K	A 2	Ace-King Deuce.
2nd " " "			6	6 6	Three Sixes.
3rd " " "			K	7 K	Two Kings.
4th " " "			8	9 J	Jack High.
6th " " "			J	8 7	Jack High.
7th " " "			2	A 5	Ace High.

The Betting

2nd hand holds Three Sixes, two of which are exposed. He bets.
3rd raises on Two Kings, according to the book.
4th, 6th, 7th and 1st players all fold.
2nd player just calls, waiting for the kill with Three Sixes.

The Deal

			One Down	Three Up	
2nd player is dealt			6	6 6 3	Three Sixes.
3rd " " "			K	7 K 9	Two Kings.

The Betting

2nd player with Two Exposed Sixes checks. He knows 3rd will bet.
3rd bets on Two Kings, taking the bait.
2nd raises with Three Sixes.
3rd should know he is trapped and should fold, but he calls.

The Deal

			One Down	Four Up	
2nd player is dealt			6	6 6 3 A	Three Sixes.
3rd " " "			K	7 K 9 8	Two Kings.

The Betting

2nd player is High with Two Exposed Sixes. He bets.
3rd player knows he is beat but is curious enough to call. It is hard to drive
    out a sucker once he has his money in the pot.

Winning Hand

Three Sixes, held by 2nd player.

MONTY'S COMMENT *Continued*

2ND DEAL

The Deal

				One Down	One Up	
1st player	is	dealt		9	9	Two Nines.
2nd	"	"	"	4	5	Five High.
3rd	"	"	"	A	J	Ace High.
4th	"	"	"	J	9	Jack High.
5th	"	"	"	7	9	Nine High.
6th	"	"	"	K	5	King High.
7th	"	"	"	8	8	Two Eights.

The Betting

3rd player is High with the Jack. He bets.

4th player calls on J-9. This is an especially poor call because two of his Nines are exposed.

5th also calls. This is a poor call for the same reason.

6th calls on K-5.

7th raises on Two Concealed Eights. He thinks more of Two Eights than I do.

1st player sees an opportunity to win a small pot and re-raises on Two Concealed Nines.

2nd, 3rd, 4th, 5th and 6th players cannot stand a double raise and fold.

7th player calls on Two Eights.

The Deal

				One Down	Two Up	
1st player	is	dealt		9	9 J	Two Nines.
7th	"	"	"	8	8 K	Two Eights.

The Betting

7th player is High with the King. He checks his Two Eights.

1st bets on Two Concealed Nines.

7th calls. He thinks he is beat, but hopes to draw out.

The Deal

				One Down	Three Up	
1st player	is	dealt		9	9 J 2	Two Nines.
7th	"	"	"	8	8 K J	Two Eights.

The Betting

7th player is High with Two Concealed Eights and the King, and checks.

1st player bets his Two Concealed Nines.

7th at last folds.

Winning Hand

Two Nines, held by 1st player.

Monty's Comment *Continued*

3rd Deal

The Deal

				One Down	One Up	
1st player	is	dealt		A	2	Ace High.
2nd	"	"	"	J	J	Two Jacks.
3rd	"	"	"	K	A	Ace High.
4th	"	"	"	Q	K	King High.
5th	"	"	"	2	3	Three High.
6th	"	"	"	5	4	Five High.
7th	"	"	"	6	3	Six High.

The Betting

3rd player is High with the Ace. He must bet and does.
4th player stays with King High.
5th, 6th and 7th players fold.

1st calls with Ace High. He should fold because 3rd player has an ace exposed.
2nd player with Two Jacks does not want to disclose his hand, and just calls.

The Deal

				One Down	Two Up	
1st player	is	dealt		A	2 3	Ace High. No change.
2nd	"	"	"	J	J 7	Two Jacks. No change.
3rd	"	"	"	K	A 6	Ace High. No change.
4th	"	"	"	Q	K 10	King High. No change.

The Betting

3rd player is High with the Ace. He bets.
4th player calls with King High.
1st player calls with the Ace.
2nd player raises with Two Jacks, hoping opponents will think he has Two Sevens.
3rd and 4th players call.
1st player folds.

The Deal

				One Down	Three Up	
2nd player	is	dealt		J	J 7 9	Two Jacks. No change.
3rd	"	"	"	K	A 6 2	Ace High. No change.
4th	"	"	"	Q	K 10 10	Two Tens. Improved.

The Betting

4th player bets with Two Tens.
2nd raises with Two Concealed Jacks.
3rd folds.
4th calls with Two Tens.

Monty's Comment *Continued*

3rd Deal (*Continued*)

The Deal

	One Down	Three Up	
2nd player is dealt	J	J 7 8 A	Two Jacks. No change.
4th " " "	Q	K 10 10 4	Two Tens. No change.

The Betting

4th player checks his Two Tens.

2nd player bets the Two Concealed Jacks.

At this stage of the game there is so much money in the pot that 4th player calls.

Winning Hand

Two Jacks, held by 2nd player.

III

Five-Card Draw, Deuces Wild with the Joker

———◆———

1.

Monty caught a fellow cheating at cards a few days later. He pretended to be a sucker when, in fact, he was cheating the life out of us, especially at stud. Some of us sensed this but couldn't spot what was going on. Monty was playing and called me into his study.

"Do you know that new guy?"

"I've seen him a couple of times. He's called One-Eye Jones. He's from Indianapolis, I think."

"Did you notice anything shady?"

"No, except that thick lens he is wearing over his good eye. I don't recall he ever wore glasses before."

Monty pulled out a deck of cards. "I put these in my pocket when we changed packs the last time." It is customary to change decks quite often—not to detect cheating, but because players become superstitious when they aren't winning, and call for a new deck.

46

Monty held the pack under a light, back up, bent half of the deck toward him, and released the cards one at a time. When he did this fast you could see the marks. They stood out like a motion picture film turned slowly.

"Just what I suspected," he said with a hearty laugh. "We sure are suckers not to spot this. One-Eye's sight must be pretty poor if he has to use magnifying glasses."

The cards, according to Monty, were professionally marked by a person who caters to crooks. In stud, One-Eye, with his magnifying glasses, could read the back of every down card around the table. No wonder we were all losers.

Monty, who was running the game, sent Runt after One-Eye and his chips. When told he'd been caught red-handed, One-Eye gave a sheepish grin.

"How did you switch decks?" asked Monty in a cold voice.

"I dropped a chip on the floor and made the switch when I picked it up."

"You crooks must think this place a soft touch," Monty said angrily. "Guess you read the penalty?" One-Eye shook his head. "I put a sign on the wall only last week warning crooks I'd throw them out on their ass and they'd forfeit their take-out and all winnings if caught. Got anything to say for yourself?"

"No—except if I have to be thrown out I'd rather Runt did it than you."

Monty gained his good humor at once. "All right, Runt. Throw him out the back way but don't be too rough."

Monty was counting One-Eye's chips. "There's a little over five hundred here."

"For a private charity, I suppose," I said slyly.

"You guessed it. It's for Lucille March."

"Lucille March!" I exclaimed. "Why, she's a drug addict. You mean her dad, a deacon in the church, would take charity from a gambler?"

"The old hypocrite will never know. I'm sending this money to her sister, who will arrange for Lucille to visit her and then enter an institution for cure."

"Well, I'll be a so-and-so, as you say. Old Doc Prittle must be pretty proud of himself with all the drug addicts he's made in town."

"That's about all he knows—morphine, quinine, and calomel. He certainly doesn't know anything about abortion and sure did a butcher's job on Lucille."

Lucille's history was no town secret. The town even knew that Chic the chicken picker was the guilty one. The town whispered that Lucille insisted on Doc's performing an operation. Complications set in and Doc gave her morphine to ease the pain.

"I hope she gets cured in Indianapolis," Monty said.

"You're a good man, Monty," I said affectionately.

Monty looked embarrassed. "You were going to talk about the poker cut," he said, changing the subject, but first he called to Jack to take over.

"Well, I have two ideas. The amount of the money you make on cutting the pots depends on how many pots there are per hour. Make an eighth place at the table and get a fast dealer to deal all the hands. A lot of time is lost with each player dealing."

"I'm afraid the boys wouldn't like that. Each man likes to deal. Besides, they'd probably suspect I had a confederate dealing me winning hands. What's the other idea?"

"Let's get two old decks and sit at the table." When this was done I passed one deck to Monty, who was sitting to my left. "Now assume I have just dealt and after the showdown am arranging the discards, preparing to shuffle them," I said. I mixed up the cards and began to gather them in, simulating an actual case. "Now you start dealing draw or stud." Monty began dealing seven-handed draw. By the time he was through dealing each imaginary person five cards, I had finished shuffling my pack, and placed it to Monty's left.

"You note," I said, "with two decks we handle the discards as we do now except that they are tossed to the dealer rather than to the player at the dealer's left. After the showdown the dealer picks up the discards and shuffles while the player to his left, you in this case, is dealing. It will speed up the deals twenty-five per cent according to my calculations with my dad's stop watch and consequently increase the cuts by a like amount."

"Excellent idea, kid. We'll start this at once. Want your share of the increased cut?" he joked.

"You're kidding me, Monty." His face was usually in repose or deadpan, but when he broke into a smile the whole room seemed to light up. "Got time to give me some fine points on deuces wild?" I asked diffidently.

"I've got time to give you hell for not raising on pat hands," he said. "You've made that mistake several times. Now, if you have a pat hand—a straight, flush or a full—and aren't in a position to raise in order to chase the timid soul, every son-of-a-bitch and his brother is going to draw against you, for as you know, these simpletons act like they're playing straight draw instead of draw with four wild deuces and the joker.

"Remember," he continued, "with five wild cards, almost anyone can open, and they do. On the other hand, in straight draw only a player with jacks or better can open. In deuces, holding a pat hand, I'd risk a passed pot rather than open. Oh, you might open if you sit just one position to the dealer's right," he concluded.

"I'll try to remember, Monty," I said in a low voice.

"Oh, don't be so sensitive about it. It's for your own good." Monty was laughing at me. "As I said, these simpletons, except for a few exceptions, open with one deuce, or a joker—two aces, two kings, three small ones—about everything in the deck. If all of them draw, you'll get beat with a pat hand. Suppose they all draw and someone bets you a hunk? What you going to do?"

"Eat them, I guess."

"Now, here's the way to play the pat hand," he continued. "Check and wait for someone to open. It is usually opened for the size of the pot, say three dollars and fifty cents."

"You forget we cut the pot fifty cents."

"Oh, dammit, don't be so technical. Suppose three stay. That's four players or about fifteen dollars in the pot, a worthwhile winning. Now bet twenty dollars or about a fifteen-dollar raise. You'll be surprised to see how many throw in the sponge. With only one or two stayers you've got a pretty good chance of winning. No one is going to back in on you after you've made a twenty-dollar bet, unless they have two wild cards or three of a kind above the ten, or at least I wouldn't.

"So your opponents draw. You stand pat. If they check, you spread. If one of them bets—well, that is a horse of another color. You're in a mouse trap. Judge your man. Has he really got the guts to bet if he can't beat a pat hand?" Monty shook his head. "Kid, I can't tell you what to do under those circumstances. You're on your own."

"Suppose under the same circumstances I raise and draw one card."

"To what?"

"To a bust—nothing."

"What are you trying to make your opponents believe?" Monty asked.

"To believe I have four of a kind and am trying to make the fifth."

Monty laughed heartily. "These simpletons will never believe you. They'll think you're drawing to a straight, flush, or two pair."

"You know I'm not simple-minded enough to draw to such cards."

"Hell, no. But the point is, do they? Oh, a strong player may fall for your idea," he added as an afterthought. "Now, kid, you're playing real good and winning us some money—that's the proof. But you still gamble with weaker hands than I do." He looked at his watch.

I asked, "Do you have time to go over again with me just what cards you stay on in deuces wild? You've given me a good lesson on the pat hand."

"Those geldings can wait just thirty minutes for poker. I've got a date."

"The smell of horses, moonlight and dew glistening on green grass?" I asked slyly.

"The smell of horses, moonlight, and *wet* dew glistening on green grass," Monty corrected with a straight face.

He had picked up a pad and was writing.

After a few moments he said, "Here, study this. It tells you what to play on, when to call, and when to raise. The x represents any card other than a face card or an ace."

A A A x x or better	Raise
K K K x x	Raise
Q Q Q x x	Call
J J J x x	Call
2A A x x or better	Raise
2K K x x	Raise
2Q Q x x	Call
2J J x x	Call
2 2 x x x or better	Raise
Straights	Raise
Flushes	Raise
Full Houses	Raise

"Never," he said emphatically, "stay with only one wild card unless you hold three jacks or better, not even *2* 10 10 x x."

I studied the list a moment. "Jesus, Monty, no wonder you told me you hadn't lost in three years, if you only stay on such strong hands. If everyone played like you do there wouldn't be a poker game."

"No, there wouldn't," Monty admitted. "When I play I either think I have the best hand or the makings of one. I'm not interested in second-best hands. Let the suckers stay on less."

"It looks like poker, as you play it, is a sort of legalized theft."

"Yes, it is," Monty said. "And only once removed from playing like a card sharp."

"We play table stakes here. You mean I can win at limit poker with these pointers you have given me?"

"What the hell's the difference whether I bet you a buck or a hundred if I think the odds favor my winning? Players who can't win at limit poker and imagine they could at table stakes are victims of wishful thinking. A sound poker player can win in *any* poker game.

"While we are on the subject of poker, I should like to give you a bit of advice," Monty continued. "One of the most important things you should do is to keep a file on all players—name, approximate age, condition of health, and obvious characteristics. Then study the players at all times for characteristics not so obvious. After a while you will get to know them like a book and can accurately determine in most cases when they help their hands and when they are trying to run a bluff.

"Though you usually play cards at the same place and among the same crowd, there will be times when you visit another club or group and may wish to play, provided the game is not too tight. A few moments' observation will tell you this. If, for example, they are playing seven-handed, and four players stay consistently, you know the game is loose because four players out of seven cannot possibly hold minimum strength consistently, as I define it. It follows therefore that a number of weak players are in the game.

"A hopeless and helpless friend of mine told me he had lost twenty-five thousand dollars during a lifetime of poker. I gave him a few lessons, then watched him play. He still tossed his money away. When I reminded him of this he simply looked confused. I said, 'You played only two hours and lost your Old Soldier's check. If you played percentages you could play every day and still have your check.' He shook his head sadly. 'I don't know, Monty,' he said. 'I guess I just like to play cards.'

"Never stay in a poker game unless there are at least three suckers. If possible, let them do your betting for you, and sit to their left because they are usually wild players who bet on everything and anything. Sitting to their left gives you the option whether to stay, raise, or fold your hand.

"I am reminded of players who insist on 'betting on the come'; that is, to bet that their next card will improve the hand. I have listened to their arguments and nodded in agreement, but I simply do not play that kind of poker unless the odds are in my favor. I figure the odds for every card I draw, and if the odds are not favorable, I fold. This doesn't sound very friendly. But what's friendly about poker? It's a cutthroat game, at best."

2.

I was eating prairie chicken at ten cents a chicken at Monty's bar about ten days later when Jack came in to tell me that he wanted relief and that he had left a vacant seat.

"Is Monty playing?"

"Yes. It's eight o'clock now. I'll be back at 2 A.M."

I went in and sat down in the chair vacated by Jack. There were two new faces. I had seen the two hanging around the tent show where they featured such plays as *Ten Nights in a Barroom, Uncle Tom's Cabin, Dr. Jekyll and Mr. Hyde,* and the like.

"Kid, you know Tom Lawrence and Pete Hunter, leading man and producer," Monty said with a sweep of his hand.

I nodded the introduction. The handsome chap sitting at Monty's left I judged to be the leading man; the other, sitting next to the actor, looked for all the world like a producer. He was chewing at a dry cigar and he grinned constantly, showing yellow teeth filled with gold inlays which glistened in the lamplight.

I sat next, then Chic the chicken picker, Doc and then Bones Alverson, the farmer, his leatherlike face beaten from exposure. I knew he had lost most of his farm at poker. Rumor had it that he had hocked everything to Bert Willis, the land speculator, known to be a ruthless and shrewd operator.

I turned to Chic. He had several stacks in front of him. "You must have sold some more dead chickens," I said in a low voice. Chic was a notoriously poor poker player and when he wasn't taking live chickens to New York he picked them dry at the poultry house for three cents a head.

He gave me a sour look. "Keep your mouth shut, you little shrimp," he warned.

The game progressed as usual—some winning, some losing. I was trying to remember all that Monty had told me, and played carefully.

Monty looked bored. Doc Prittle nodded in his seat between deals, his head resting on his double chin. Bones Alverson was getting some good hands and was winning consistently. The actor and his backer seemed alert and were holding their own.

The game droned on. I got up and stretched my legs to relieve my nervousness. I don't know what it was but I had a feeling of impending tragedy. And it wasn't long in coming.

Doc Prittle was fumbling with the deck. He had put in the joker preparatory to dealing deuces wild and was awkwardly reshuffling the cards.

Monty watched him in disgust. "Deal, goddammit, Doc."

Startled, Doc yelled back, "Hold your horses," then, after taking his time, began to deal five-card draw deuces wild.

Bones, the farmer, skinned back his cards in his gnarled hands. I imagined I saw a flicker in his eyes. Anyway he made an unusual opening bet. He bet $50 right under the gun.

Monty, sitting next, studied Bones for a fleeting moment, then folded. He later told me he held a jack full.

The actor tossed his hand in the discards in disgust.

But his producer was grinning impishly. "I raise one hundred," he said and tossed in the chips.

I threw my hand in the discards, as did also Chic and Doc, the dealer. Looks like those two had all the wild cards, I reflected.

Bones pretended to study a moment, then counted out a big stack of chips, for he had been winning. "I up you five hundred," he said, his voice quivering.

Bones had a mouthful of tobacco juice and was watching the producer intently. I could see he was afraid to turn his head to spit. He made the motion to do so, but changed his mind and swallowed tobacco cud, juice and all. He choked a bit, and pulled out a red handkerchief and wiped his mouth.

Monty, seeing the play, cried the usual "I'll be a son-of-a-bitch."

Bones choked again. "Well," he said to the grinning producer, "what the hell you going to do?"

The producer took out a sheaf of hundred-dollar bills. "I'm just going to raise you five hundred."

"Raise you five hundred more," Bones quivered, "you city prick." He turned to Monty. "Put in one thousand, Monty," he said. Monty demurred. "You've never seen me welch on a bet," Bones pleaded.

"No, I never did," said Monty thoughtfully. "But you used to have a farm. Do you have one now?"

"I'll tell you the God's own truth, Monty," he said. "I've got the farm, stock and implements plastered to Bert Wills for fifteen thousand. Bert offered me twenty thousand. So I have five thousand equity."

Monty shook his head sadly. "Bones, let me give you some friendly advice. Just call him. I'll lend you money for that."

"Call, hell!" exclaimed Bones. "This is a chance of a lifetime. Loan me the thousand. I want to raise the bastard."

"I can't understand you, Bones. You've lost three-fourths of your farm and now you want to bet the last fourth."

"Goddammit, yes. I might just as well be broke as to try to pay ten per cent interest on fifteen thousand to that goddamned bloodsucker."

"Jesus," said Monty, "I don't mind risking the thousand but—"

"You ain't risking nothing, goddammit. I've got him beat."

"All right. But just give me first chance to buy the farm if you do lose." Monty tossed two five-hundred-dollar bills in the pot and took Bones's IOU.

The producer had lost his grin. Even the unlighted cigar had disappeared somehow. He reached for his purse and spread five hundred-dollar bills and pushed them in the pot.

He said in a subdued voice, "There's my five hundred and I raise two thousand. I'll have to give you an IOU."

"You will in a pig's ass. Go get it."

"How can I? The banks are closed."

"You ain't got no two thousand in the bank. Put up or shut up," said Bones.

"Monty, will you take my IOU?" asked the producer.

"Let me tell you bastards something," Monty replied. "I'm not financing this poker game. I'm just playing in it. If I'd wanted to stay

I'd have stayed and financed myself if I got in trouble. And another thing. You bastards slow up a game. I only get fifty cents cut. This one I should cut five hundred."

No one offered to agree to this but I had a sneaking feeling that Monty was going to profit in this transaction somehow.

The producer placed some chips on his cards resting on the table and got up and pulled along the actor with him. They went in the other end of the room and I couldn't hear what they said, but the actor was protesting and the producer was really telling it to him Finally, they both sat down.

The producer addressed Monty. "You know my reputation. You know I own three other tent shows and I can tell you I don't owe a dime on them. My leading man here owns one-third of this show. I'd like to own that farm even if it is mortgaged."

"Well," said Monty, "what's your proposition?"

"This farmer gave you an IOU for one thousand. Put it in the pot and take out one thousand in cash. That makes you square. I'll make out a bill of sale for my show for two thousand, if this farmer will make out a bill of sale for his farm for three thousand. The extra thousand covers the money you take from the pot."

"Bones, do you understand the deal?" asked Monty.

"Is the show worth two thousand?"

"I'd like to own it for that."

"But I'm pledging three thousand and my equity is five thousand."

"You'll get the difference if you lose."

"Goddammit, I'm not going to lose. I'd like to own a show. More money in it than following a plow around a field, I reckon."

"It's your funeral," said Monty prophetically, and directed Runt to bring in bills of sale, pen and ink. When Monty looked over the papers he pointed out that the producer's bill of sale needed the actor's signature because of a one-third interest. He put Bones's IOU in the pot and took out a thousand according to the agreement.

"Just a minute, Monty. I didn't pledge my prize bull. Nobody's going to plaster him with a mortgage."

"He'll get plastered if you fill your hand." Monty laughed. "How many cards you want, Bones? You take cards first."

"I want one," Bones said and tossed his discard toward Doc.

Doc was so nervous he could scarcely get a card off the top of the deck. Monty didn't help much by yelling at him. Doc finally flicked a card face down toward Bones. It touched Bones's hand, bounced; then turned over, exposed. I looked at it horror-stricken, for I had said a little prayer for Bones.

It was the joker.

"I'm sorry, Bones," said Doc.

Bones opened his mouth as if to protest, but no sound came. He just sat there fascinated and stared at the joker who, I thought, stared impishly back at him. Then a deep pallor began to creep slowly over Bones's weather-beaten face.

"What'll I do, Monty? Can't Bones take the joker?"

"No. If you'd read the rules you'd know he can't. They're all printed and framed on the wall behind you. You deal whatever cards the producer wants to him, then Bones gets the next card. Tough luck, Bones."

The pallor had spread over Bones's face. His eyes looked glazed. Suddenly he fell over the table, clutching the cards in his heavy fist.

At this Doc jumped up, handing me the deck. He examined Bones for several seconds. At last he said, "He's dead, boys."

An air of disbelief settled over the players. Even Monty was speechless for the moment, then, "You're sure, Doc?" he asked.

"Yes, I'm sure. His heart stopped. Too much excitement. I guess I killed him."

The producer made a pass at the pot, starting to rake it in. Monty's fist reached out and nearly broke the showman's wrist. "Hands off!" Monty snarled.

"It's mine," protested the producer.

"Not yet, my friend," Monty said softly. "I think he had you beat. He didn't need the joker."

"Well, I don't think so, and I demand to draw to my hand," said the producer.

"Kid," asked Monty, "has the deck been disturbed?"

"No. Doc handed it to me."

"Well, I'm going to write a new rule that Hoyle didn't cover. If you fellows agree, I'll rule we let our producer draw to his hand, then take Bones's cards from his fist and add the next card to it." They all nodded agreement except the producer, who protested feebly.

"How many cards you want?" asked Monty.

"One," said the producer.

"Kid, give him a card."

The producer threw me the discard and I gave him one, face down.

By that time Doc had pried Bones's cards from his huge fist, so I slipped Doc a card to fill out the hand.

"Now wait a moment, boys," said Monty. "Who wants to bet on the winning hand?"

The actor was the only one to answer. "I've got five hundred that says my producer wins."

"Covered," said Monty, tossing the money on the table. The producer spread his hand. He held Q K K K 2. "Four Kings," said Monty.

Doc turned over Bones's cards one at a time, calling them out as he did so. "Ace, ace, ace, jack, deuce—four aces."

"You ran second," Monty said to the producer. "That's irony for you. A man dies holding the winning hand—" and he picked up the actor's bet. Then he began to rake in the pot. "I'll take this to Bones's widow. She'll probably grieve a couple of days, then be relieved that he's dead. At least he can't gamble the farm away now."

The producer said, "I'll redeem that bill of sale, Monty, when the banks open."

"You will like hell," said Monty. "I'll redeem it myself if the widow consents. I've always wanted to go in show business."

3. MONTY'S COMMENT: *Summary of Deuces Wild*

This will teach you to win either at limit poker or table stakes.

WHAT TO STAY ON
See page 51

THE PLAY
(I have dealt four hands as exercises)

1ST DEAL

After the Deal

1st player is dealt	2 2 5 5 4	Two Deuces or Four Fives.
2nd	"	"	"	2 J 10 5 3	One Deuce or Two Jacks
3rd	"	"	"	5 6 7 8 9	Nine High Straight.
4th	"	"	"	A A 9 8 7	Two Aces.
5th	"	"	"	a bust.
6th	"	"	"	" "
*7th	"	"	"	2 J 8 5 4	One Deuce or Two Jacks.

     * The Dealer.

The Betting

1st opens with Two Deuces or Four Fives.
2nd stays on One Deuce or Two Jacks. Never stay on One Wild Card.
3rd raises on a Nine High Straight.
4th, 5th, 6th and 7th hands fold.

1st and 2nd hands stay.

After the Draw

1st player throws away the Two Fives and draws to Two Deuces. Makes
        2 2 A K Q—Ace High Straight.
2nd player draws Four to the Deuce. Makes 2 K Q 9 7—Two Kings.
3rd player stands pat on a Nine High Straight.

The Betting

1st player checks an Ace High Straight. He's afraid of the Pat Hand.
2nd checks Two Kings.
3rd checks a Small Straight.

Winning Hand

Ace High Straight, held by 1st player.

2ND DEAL

The Deal

1st player is dealt 2 3 6 8 9 A Single Deuce. He is permitted to draw
                                          Four.
2nd " " " a bust.
3rd " " " 3 4 5 6 10 A 4-Card Straight.

Monty's Comment *Continued*

2ND DEAL (*Continued*)

4th	"	"	"	2 Q Q 7 4	Three Queens.
5th	"	"	"	2 K K 6 5	Three Kings.
6th	"	"	"	2 A A 8 6	Three Aces.
*7th	"	"	"	a bust.	

* The Dealer.

The Betting

1st, 2nd and 3rd players do not have openers.
4th player opens on Three Queens.
5th raises on Three Kings.
6th re-raises on Three Aces.

7th, 1st, 2nd and 3rd players fold.
4th stands the re-raise. A questionable play.
5th stays. Also a questionable play.

After the Draw

4th draws Two to 2 Q Q.	Makes	2 Q Q K 3	Three Queens. No change.
5th	"	"	" 2 K K.	"	2 K K J 6	No change.
6th	"	"	" 2 A A.	"	2 A A 8 7	No change.

The Betting

4th player checks Three Queens.
5th checks Three Kings.
6th bets the Three Aces, 4th and 5th players having checked.

4th player folds Three Queens.
5th calls on Three Kings.

Winning Hand

Three Aces, held by 6th player.

3RD DEAL

The Deal

1st player is dealt	2 A 7 4 3	Two Aces. He will open and draw to Two Aces, a sucker play. He should never open or even stay with less than Three Jacks or a Full Hand. Two Wild Cards, of course, is a very strong hand.
2nd	"	"	"	Q Q 6 5 4	Two Queens.
3rd	"	"	"	2 2 A 6 5	Three Aces.
4th	"	"	"	a bust	
5th	"	"	"	" "	
6th	"	"	"	" "	
*7th	"	"	"	J J J 4 3	Three Natural Jacks.

* The Dealer

Monty's Comment *Continued*

3rd Deal (*Continued*)

The Betting

1st opens with Two Aces.

2nd stays on Two Queens. Such optimism is admirable but if he continues to play like this he will go broke.

3rd raises on Three Aces.

4th, 5th and 6th hands fold.

7th calls on Three Jacks—a very questionable play.

1st player stays on Two Aces, sending good money after bad.

2nd also calls. One never ceases to wonder at calls on such weak hands.

After the Draw

1st draws Three cards.			Makes	2 A K Q 10	Ace High Straight.
2nd "	"	"	"	Q Q J 9 8	No change. Two Queens.
3rd "	Two	"	"	2 A A 2 7	Four Aces.
7th "	"	"	"	J J J 3 4	Three Jacks. No change.

The Betting

1st checks the Ace High Straight.

2nd checks Two Queens.

3rd bets with Four Aces.

7th folds Three Jacks.

1st calls with Ace High Straight.

2nd folds.

Winning Hand

Four Aces, held by 3rd player.

4th Deal

The Deal

1st player is dealt			a bust.		
2nd "	"	"	2 8 8 A Q	Single Deuce or Three Eights.
3rd "	"	"	9 9 9 K 6	Three Natural Nines.
4th "	"	"	a bust.	
5th "	"	"	2 4 5 6 7	Eight High Straight.
6th "	"	"	2 3 4 5 9	Single Deuce.
*7th "	"	"	a bust.	

    * The Dealer.

The Betting

1st player checks a bust.

2nd opens on Three Eights. I need Three Jacks to open but I wouldn't open at all unless I was sitting close to the Dealer's right. This game has Five Wild cards so there is no worry about passing up a good hand, for nearly all pots are opened—mostly, of course, on weak hands.

Monty's Comment *Continued*

4th Deal (*Continued*)

3rd stays on Three Natural Nines. The reason this game is so easily beat is
because players are so eager to throw away money on hands that percentage players would toss in the discards.

4th folds a bust.

5th raises on an Eight High Straight.

6th and 7th fold.

1st folds.

2nd and 3rd players stay on weak hands.

After the Draw

2nd player draws Two to Three Eights. Makes 2 8 8 5 3   No change.

3rd   "   "   "   " Three Nines.   "   9 9 9 A K   No change.

5th stands pat on Eight High Straight.

The Betting

2nd player checks Three Eights.

3rd checks Three Nines.

5th checks a Straight. He is satisfied to check since it just may be possible that
the 2nd or 3rd hands might have made Four of a Kind.

Winning Hand

Straight, held by 5th player.

Part Two

THREE POKER STORIES

I

Five-Card Draw, Low Ball

———◆————————————————————

1.

I did not fulfill my ambition to become a criminal lawyer. Instead, I landed in the code room of the Department of State. Later, when World War I broke out, I organized a deciphering bureau to read intercepted enemy messages—the first of its kind since the Civil War. I had about 160 men and women under me. During the war and after, until the bureau was closed by a naïve President, we deciphered around 200,000 messages to and from such nations as Japan, Germany, England, France, Mexico and all South American countries. I had received the Distinguished Service Medal for being the first to break the Japanese diplomatic cipher.

In the 30s I had written a book about my experiences. Upon the publication of *The American Black Chamber,* with its revelation of Japanese intrigue, I became a marked man in the Orient, and the Chinese authorities who had engaged me to organize a Chinese cipher bureau therefore decided to smuggle me in under the name of Herbert Osborn to avoid recognition and possible assassination by the Japanese.

I choose China as the locale for the remainder of my story about how I win at poker because poker was instrumental in catching a secret agent whose mission was either to assassinate or to capture the Generalissimo.

At Hong Kong I was met by my interpreter, Ling Fan, who was well supplied with money and instructed to provide everything for my comfort. He was a little man with a yellow skin, dressed in foreign clothes; his black hair was parted at the side and brushed back.

My advance reputation was formidable and I had the difficult task of trying to live up to it. My resourcefulness was put to the test almost at once.

Ling and I were drinking Scotch and soda in the Hong Kong Hotel cocktail room and watching the beautiful and well-dressed Chinese women in their long colored silk gowns, some split above the knee. I was about to put to Ling a question about the charms of Chinese women when he asked, a bit diffidently, "Advisor, is it really true that a white woman's breasts are red?" When I didn't answer at once he explained, "That's what a returned Chinese student from Paris told me."

"Is that all he told you?" I asked.

"Well, no," he said with some hesitation. "He also told me—I don't know what you call it in English—but he told me it was also red."

Clearly it was up to me to show myself all-wise and all-powerful. I promised Ling to procure him a look-see, and to that end we set out upon my first assignment, surely a curious one for the foreign advisor in ciphers and counterespionage for the government in Chungking.

I pushed Ling into a taxi and directed the driver to go to the police station. Ling was somewhat perturbed at this but more fascinated by the operation of the taximeter.

At the police station I went in alone and put my question to the pompous English Colonel in charge: "Where can I find a white prostitute in Hong Kong?"

The Colonel puffed up like a toad, told me there was none such, and if there were, the authorities would jolly well chase her out. I knew he was either a fool or lying. However, there was nothing to do but go. One of his Irish subordinates followed me out and gave me the desired address. There were two white prostitutes, he said, in the city—French, and quite nice too.

I left Ling in the taxi. The apartment, presided over by a fat and rouged madam, was on one of the hills overlooking the bay. The madam and I conducted preliminary negotiations in a stuffy drawing room over port and Scotch and soda. An attractive brunette and a pretty blonde appeared. I explained in inadequate French that I was on my way to interior China. One, or both for that matter, could do me a great favor. They smiled their willingness. Then I pulled a sheaf of Hong Kong hundred-dollar bills from my coat pocket. I could well afford to be generous, for Ling had given me $1,000 Hong Kong when he met me at the boat—a little gift from my future boss, the Hatchet Man, with which to amuse myself while in Hong Kong. I extracted two bills and replaced the others. Three Hong Kong dollars equalled one in our money.

I was too new in the Orient to be sure of the status of the yellow man among white prostitutes and so told my story, experimentally, about a friend of mine—he didn't wish to go to bed with them, merely wanted to see them *au naturel*. Would they undress before him?

They must have thought me crazy, for they looked at each other and laughed gustily. Then they wanted to know if I was the "friend."

I said, "No, he's my Chinese interpreter."

"*Le chien!*" they cried and spat.

I found myself outside and lying to the expectant Ling. I succeeded in putting him off. But my responsibility was only deferred. Face must be saved and the Honorable Advisor proved to be infallible.

I got my chance later in Haiphong where the Hatchet Man's undercover agent met our freighter and bribed us past the customs. My phony passport was not challenged and now I could relax. There would be no difficulties at the Chinese border. I had been upset by the prospect of being picked up by the police for registering under a false name, carrying concealed weapons, an aviation radio direction finder, and three suitcases filled with brochures on espionage, codes and ciphers. The aggregate sentence for these offenses would doubtless exceed my life's expectancy.

The undercover agent was instrumental in my saving face with Ling, whom I had disappointed in the affair of the French ladies in Hong Kong. Through the agent I called on a French manicurist, a friend of the police commissioner, I was told. Surprisingly enough she agreed to the proposal I made her, and Ling's curiosity was satisfied. As a consequence I now stood high in his eyes and was unquestionably destined to be a great man in China.

Ling had covered his original disappointment by asking whether I played poker. When I said yes, he told me there was usually a pretty good game at the Foreign Club. I must have looked doubtful for he assured me he would get me in. It appears that the omnipotent Hatchet Man had anticipated our being bored with the delays in Hong Kong and had arranged for Ling to become a member. Ling told me later that he had played poker with the foreigners in Hankow before the Chungking Government had moved further inland to Chungking.

They played dealer's choice at the Club—draw, stud, deuces wild, seven-card stud, low ball, Hi-Lo, spit-in-the-ocean, and all the other bastard poker games unknown to me in my boyhood.

Never in my life have I seen such utter disregard for money as Ling displayed, and never have I seen such poor poker played. The game, as usual, was composed mostly of simpletons but Ling was no match for even their slovenly play. I got up at the end of an hour to cut his losses. I had won about $500 Hong Kong and Ling had easily lost $1,000.

I didn't say a word until we got in our hotel room and poured two drinks. "Ling," I said at last, "I've played poker in more places than you can count, but you are the goddamnest sucker I ever saw."

"Sucker?" he said. "That's a fish," and he pulled from his pocket his small dictionary he always carried and looked it up.

"So it is." I laughed in spite of myself. "Look up simpleton."

He thumbed the pages and read, "Simpleton—a person lacking in common sense; a silly person; a fool."

"We call a simpleton a sucker, or a fish, as you suggest."

"You mean because I lost? I always lose. Haven't won in six months."

I didn't ask him what he used for money. That I learned much later in Chungking. Gasoline was rationed there but the Honorable Advisor could have all he wanted. It was delivered to me in fifty-gallon drums but from the mileage on the car I suspected that I, or rather the Service, was getting cheated. It was true. There was a six-inch air space at the top of each drum. I asked the manager of APC, Asiatic Petroleum Corporation, whether this was too much space.

"Yes," he told me, "one inch is enough. Someone is stealing five gallons out of each drum before you get it and probably selling it on the black market for two hundred fifty dollars Chinese or twenty-five dollars Gold. Multiply this by hundreds of thousands of drums and you get into real money."

"I'll report this to my superiors," I said. He advised me seriously against doing so. Then it came home to me that this was not the petty graft of small fry but a gigantic squeeze by government officials reminiscent of official theft in America. What slice Ling got, and for how many drums, I did not know, though I learned later that his father was high in the councils of the Generalissimo.

I talked to Ling about this later. He was amused. "Small thief if caught is executed," he said. "If successful he becomes an honored official and bigger theft becomes a prerequisite of office." Which philosophy recalls Western wisdom both ancient and modern, to the same effect. Nor did it seem to me on mature thought that I was the one to initiate reforms in China.

I said to Ling, "You ought to throw away that goddamned dictionary you're always studying and learn how to play poker. How did you learn to speak English anyway?"

"I studied English under a priest," he said. "I told him I was a Christian. English lessons for Buddhists cost five dollars. For Christians only one dollar."

"The propaganda minister," I said, "tells us the Generalissimo is a Christian and reads the Bible every day."

"The propaganda minister also gives out"—and Ling smiled sardonically—"that America loans the Chinese fifty million gold dollars."

"Ling," I said severely, "I didn't know hypocrisy was a Chinese characteristic."

He shrugged. "Ancient ancestor say, 'Crows are black everywhere.' " When he let this sink in he said, "You serious about teaching me poker? You win often?"

"I very seldom lose."

"You believe in Jesus Christ?"

Startled, I looked at Ling's impassive face for some sign of why he asked. Suddenly I knew why foreigners speak of the Oriental as being inscrutable. It was his eyes. They had the same expression as Ruddy Flew's, our home town baseball pitcher, who lost his eyelashes when he contracted syphilis.

"Missionaries have been good to you," I said. "They taught you English at cut rates. They teach you hygiene for nothing. Isn't that enough? What does it matter whether Buddhism or Christianity is the true religion?"

"But the missionaries come with the Bible in one hand and rice in the other."

"Then eat the rice."

Said Ling, "It is true even as ancient wisdom says that beggars cannot be choosers, but in America I imagine none is so poor as to swallow Buddhism with rice."

"Then," I advised him, "swallow the rice only and don't go around asking people if they believe in Jesus Christ." Later I was to learn that Chinese students everywhere asked foreigners the same question.

It was late so we turned in. I took care to see that my money belt was concealed beneath my pajamas. It contained $2,000 United States money in hundred-dollar bills. I called it my escape money. I was on my way to interior China, facing the unknown beyond the Japanese lines, and had no intention of being trapped there without funds. The money later served a dramatic purpose.

The next morning we were on our way to the tailor's, where I had ordered several suits of clothes. The tailor, while fitting me, began to jabber to Ling.

"What does he say?" I asked.

Ling spat judiciously, Western style. "He wants to know what side of your trousers you wear your waterspout."

"Well, I'll be a son-of-a-bitch," I said, imitating Monty after all these years. "Tell the bastard he flatters me."

Ling bought a deck of cards, and at the hotel I began his first lesson in poker. Old Monty, if he were still alive, would have enjoyed seeing the Honorable Advisor teaching the yellow man.

"I thought you Chinese liked to play mah-jongg," I offered.

"We do, but I like to play poker better."

"You mean play *at* it," I said and riffled the cards and dealt five each to seven imaginary players. "First, I'll teach you the easiest game in the deck, five-card low draw. You understand how it's played?"

"Sure," said Ling. "A 2 3 4 5 is the *lowest* hand, called the wheel. It is actually a straight but in low ball it is not counted as a straight." Ling turned over the first hand I had dealt and I arranged the cards in sequence: A 3 8 J Q.

"How many cards do you take to that hand?" I asked.

"I throw away the jack and queen and draw two cards to the A 3 8."

I dealt him two cards. The hand now read: A 3 8 A K.

"That's no good," said Ling. "I made a pair of aces."

"Yes, you did, and you're trying to make a low hand and not a high one. That's lesson number one. In low ball never draw more than one card. If you have to draw more than one, throw in your hand. The four cards you draw to must be lower than a nine and with no pair, such as 2 3 5 6 K, A 4 5 8 8, A 2 6 7 J, and the like."

Ling blinked his lashless eyes.

"Now take paper and pencil," I said, "and write these hands down for future study."

"No need," he said rather proudly. "I remember what I see. I have a photographic mind."

"Then if you'll discipline yourself to be patient and wait for a good hand, I'll make an amateur-professional out of you."

"What's that?"

"A player who wins."

"I'd like that, but I almost never do," Ling said sadly.

The second hand Ling turned over was A 2 J Q K.

"I would draw three cards to that," said Ling, "if you hadn't told me never to draw more than one."

"Yes, I saw you drawing three cards last night. That hand is a bust and should be folded."

"What's that?"

"A bust is a useless hand, and folded means to throw your hand in the discards."

The third hand, 5 6 6 J Q, was declared to be a bust by Ling.

The fourth hand showed 2 3 4 8 4.

"I know how to play that," Ling said. "Throw away the 4 and draw one." I dealt him the 7, making 2 3 4 7 8.

"I bet on that hand," said Ling.

The fifth hand read 2 4 5 6 K.

"I throw away the king and draw one," he said. I dealt him one card, the jack, making 2 4 5 6 J. "I bet on that hand too," he said.

"You're wrong unless you intend to bluff. Jack low is not a winning hand. If someone bets you should fold unless you suspect you're being bluffed. Nine low may be good enough to call on but not to bet. Eight low, such as the fourth hand, 2 3 4 7 8, is a betting hand."

The sixth hand was a bust, reading 7 8 9 J K.

The seventh read 3 6 7 7 K.

"I'd throw away the 7 and king and draw two," said Ling, unconvinced that a player should never draw more than one card.

I dealt him 3 10, making 3 6 7 3 10. Ling had paired, making his hand useless.

I picked up a sheet of hotel stationery and recorded the hands and the draws, with my comments. It read:

- (1) A 3 8 J Q. Ling discarded two and made A 3 8 A K, a bust.
- (2) A 2 J Q K. A bust.
- (3) 5 6 6 J Q. A bust.
- (4) 2 3 4 8 4. Ling discarded the 4 and made 2 3 4 7 8, a betting hand.
- (5) 2 4 5 6 K. Ling discarded the K and made 2 3 5 6 J, a losing hand.
- (6) 7 8 9 J K. A bust.
- (7) 3 6 7 7 K. Ling discarded two and made 3 6 7 3 10, a bust.

"I get the point," said Ling going over the list.

I dealt seven more hands and recorded them:

- (1) 4 5 8 10 J
- (2) A 5 K K K
- (3) 7 9 J J Q
- (4) 2 3 4 6 9
- (5) 2 6 7 9 J
- (6) 2 3 5 6 K
- (7) A 5 8 Q Q

"Now," I said, handing Ling the list, "tell me what you do with each hand."

"The first hand has only three cards below a nine. I would have to draw two, which you intimated is a sucker play. The second has only two cards below a nine, and therefore a bust. The third is obviously a bust. Even I wouldn't draw to it. The fourth has four cards below a nine. I draw one."

"No," I corrected. "You have a pretty fair pat hand with 2 3 4 6 9. You will ordinarily beat the simpletons who draw two cards. Against a one-card draw you have two chances to one that you win. Call if they bet you after the draw. Bet if they check to you."

Ling nodded that he understood.

"The fifth hand has three cards below a nine. The fish draws two. The sixth, I draw one. The seventh has three cards below a nine. Suckers draw two."

"Well put," I said, laughing. "Now let us try another series of hands":

(1) A 2 3 5 8
(2) 3 6 7 J K
(3) 2 4 5 9 K
(4) A 2 3 4 J
(5) 4 5 6 J Q
(6) 5 7 9 Q K
(7) 4 8 10 10 J

I showed Ling the list. He said, "I stand pat on the first."

"Yes, it is a good pat hand and should be bet both before and after the draw."

"The second," Ling said, "has three cards below a nine. If I was a sucker I'd draw two. The third also has three below a nine. The sucker draws two. I would fold. The fourth has four below a nine. I draw one card. The fifth has three below a nine. The sucker draws two. The sixth has two below a nine. It is a bust. The seventh also has only two below a nine—a bust."

"You're learning. Now let's try just one more." And I riffled the cards and dealt another seven hands. They were:

(1) 6 8 10 J Q
(2) A 2 3 4 K
(3) 2 4 8 10 10
(4) 4 5 7 8 9
(5) A 6 6 7 7
(6) A 4 5 J Q
(7) A 3 5 6 7

"The first hand is a bust," said Ling. "The second, I draw one. I have a chance to make the Wheel if I draw a 5. The third, the sucker draws two. The fourth is a pat hand. If the pot has been opened I raise. The fifth has three cards below a nine. The sucker draws two. The sixth also has three cards below a nine. The seventh looks like a very good pat hand. I would re-raise on it."

"Very, very good," I said. "Now why don't you practice what you've learned while I take on a few drinks before tiffin. Deal out seven hands. You stay on pat hands or hands in which you have to draw only one. The other hands you play like you did last night; that is, draw two or three if necessary. Keep a record of how many times you win and how many times the simpletons win. In other words, convince yourself that the type of play I have taught is winning poker."

I didn't get back until nearly two o'clock. Ling was still dealing. He looked up at me with a pleased smile.

"How'd you make out with your make-believe poker?" I asked.

"Well," he said, "the suckers are still losing and I'm still winning."

2.

We took off by airplane from Haiphong about ten days later and landed at Chungking and were driven by car up the steep cliffs to a chateau, my future home and office, situated on the Chungking promontory overlooking the muddy waters of the Yangtze and the airfield where I had landed. The chateau was, I am told, the former home of Chungking's mayor, who was mysteriously dispossessed just before my coming. There were some twenty rooms, pine floored and with unpainted plastered walls. The windows were draped with ugly blackout curtains. There were no bathrooms, fireplaces, or stoves except for the earthen charcoal ranges in the basement used for cooking. My bedroom and sitting room were on the top floor of the east wing. For furniture I had a Western bed with a thin cotton mat in lieu of springs; a washstand with bowl and pitcher, a few chairs, a settee and a commode. Though there was electricity, the lines were so taxed that even a 200-watt light was dim. The chateau was infested with huge rats. They galloped in the attic and at night became bolder and overran the rooms.

Even primitive living in my youth had not prepared me for this. I was depressed, and deep within me there stirred dark premonitions of evil to come. The wireless which arrived from the Hatchet Man did nothing to dispel this oppression. Ling translated it for me:

HONORABLE ADVISOR:
Your coming to China is highly appreciated. I would come up to Chungking to meet you were I not preoccupied with military matters which I regret. Now that you are living in Chungking I am concerned to know whether food and quarters are suitable. The Generalissimo is directing operations at the front and will not be able to come up to Chungking for the time being. But when he does come I shall come too. Then I will call on you and take you to see him.
With cordial regards, etc., etc.

About thirty young students arrived dressed in their blue Chinese gowns and were quartered in the old servants' grounds and fed from the chateau's kitchen. They were under strict military discipline and left the grounds only on a pass. Ling said they were paid $30 Chinese which is $3 gold per month.

"No poker for them?" I suggested.

"Oh, they all gamble. Chinese checkers," Ling informed me.

I began a series of lectures on codes and ciphers, Ling translating, and worked at night examining a number of captured documents brought from Hankow by one of the Hatchet Man's henchmen, my immediate superior. Since their names are taboo (the usual Chinese secret), Ling dubbed the Hatchet Man as Number One and my superior as Number Two.

Number Two, a general who had never smelled gunpowder, was dressed in a khaki uniform with a high collar and long trousers, leather shoulder strap and belt, and on the left side a sheath with a short sword. He was possibly thirty-five years of age, fat and short. He had long ears like most Chinese and a round moonface. My first impression was that he was none too intelligent.

With much ceremony Ling introduced me, and after the usual polite inquiries I told him, Ling translating, what I would require in the way of radio equipment for interception of Japanese messages, direction finders to locate enemy stations, books, maps, and dictionaries for the research department, and a number of Chinese scholars who could translate Japanese. Also I told him that I must have daily battle reports so that we could familiarize ourselves with place names of mountains, rivers, and towns; and the Japanese and Chinese armies' corps and division names as well as their commanders. He should, I told him, delegate one man from Headquarters to keep a battle map up to date. Chinese operators had already begun to intercept Japanese messages.

He made notes and after a long and flattering speech rose to go.

"My general has instructed me to place all facilities at your disposal," he said.

"My greatest wish right now is for captured documents," I told him.

"I had almost forgotten," he answered. "I brought some more with me from Hankow."

When his servant had procured them for me I examined them eagerly. It was valuable material, especially so if prisoners had been taken who could facilitate its interpretation. Prisoners do not always talk and Japanese prisoners were especially likely to be difficult, but I had come prepared for this through the use of Sodium Amytal, a harmless drug successfully used in the Crime Detection Bureau at Northwestern University. In America its indiscriminate use on criminals was illegal, but in China the Hatchet Man would, I was sure, impose no difficulties.

"You must dispatch a messenger at once," I said, "and bring to Chungking all prisoners captured with these documents."

Ling translated and Number Two stared stupidly at me. Ling's lips curled in a contemptuous sneer as he translated the reply.

"The general says that will be impossible. The prisoners have all been executed." Thereafter Number Two was dubbed the Donkey.

I was at my desk, bathing my right eye, which had become infected, in hot salt water and Ling was translating the day's afternoon sheet, presumptuously called a newspaper, when the Hatchet Man came in unannounced.

"It's Number One!" Ling whispered.

I rose and the Hatchet Man bowed, while Ling performed the customarily elaborate introduction. He was dressed in the blue-black, high-collared uniform of the party. Perhaps forty, gimlet-eyed, and of medium stature, he wore his unruly hair cut foreign style and parted at the side. He carried himself with the air of one who has power and uses it intelligently and ruthlessly. That he was the most feared man in China I could well believe. He was to the Generalissimo what Himmler was to Der Führer.

"The General says," Ling translated, "that he is happy to see you in China. The General wishes to apologize for your quarters. He is having a foreign chef flown in from Hong Kong for you. He says he will also have an eye specialist flown in. He is much concerned about your health."

Not to be outdone I replied, "Tell the General I am happy to be in China to work under his distinguished direction. I am regaining the sight of my eye, and my quarters and food are all that can be desired. Tell him that food means nothing to me and that my only wish is to be of service to China."

The Hatchet Man smiled faintly at this and looked at his wrist watch. "He says," Ling translated, "that we have an appointment with our Leader."

Most of the headquarters buildings were downtown, but the Hatchet Man's car headed for the suburbs, we following in another car. At the edge of the city we turned up a hill and stopped before a two-story gray brick house behind a high brick wall. Along the wall were lookouts with a few armed sentries.

We were admitted at once. The house itself, of perhaps ten rooms, was unpretentious. The floor was covered with small, cheap native rugs. The walls were painted white and the windows shaded with blackout cloth. There were no flowers, pictures, or scrolls.

Finally, a Chinese opened a door, bowed, and Ling and the General motioned me to precede them. We followed the Chinese down the hall a few steps and into a large, simply furnished room. At the far end in front of a cushioned chair stood a thin man in yellow khaki wearing black cloth Chinese slippers. He wore no military belt, decorations, or insignia of any kind.

I paused in the doorway awaiting some signal. He bowed his head slightly and motioned with his hand indicating a couch. There was no word spoken, no introduction. I stood momentarily to his right. He motioned for me to be seated, then to Ling and the Hatchet Man.

I was seated within three feet of the Generalissimo and so was able to observe him closely. His hair was cropped at the sides and was perhaps no longer than half an inch on top of his head. His graying mustache was closely cut. I felt that I was in the presence of a scholar or a sage rather than a great military leader.

He looked directly into my eyes and spoke, Ling translating. "The Generalissimo asks if this is your first visit to China."

I told him yes, but that I had read a great deal about China. After this was translated he looked at me again and spoke. Ling translated, "The Generalissimo says he has heard about you for many years."

I thought to myself, he's read the Chinese version of my book, *The American Black Chamber*, for which I had received not a penny in Chinese royalties. However this seemed neither the time nor the place to mention that, and so I said to Ling, "Even the school children in America know about the Generalissimo and Madame Chiang." As Ling translated, a pleased smile spread over the Generalissimo's face.

Evidently a definite routine of polite palaver introduces the conversations of Chinese officials with foreigners, for this followed a pattern to which I was accustomed. He asked me polite questions about my welfare and I think he meant it when he said, "If at any time you are not comfortable you must come and tell me."

He then asked me about my work and listened attentively while I answered, interrupting me now and then with a shrewd question. At last he glanced at a sheet of paper on a small table at his right—other appointments, I guessed—rose, gave my hand a firm grasp, bowed, and smiled. At the door I paused, and emulating my Chinese companions, bowed. He was still standing, a frail and rather lonesome man, or so he seemed to me.

The servants bowed us through the door, the sentries at the gate saluted, and as we drove away a small squad of soldiers arrived—a change of guards, I imagined.

At the time I met this great man I did not dream that I would be instrumental in frustrating a plot to assassinate or kidnap him.

II

Seven-Card Stud

————— ◆ —————————————————————————————————

1.

At the Chungking Hostel the servant told us a poker game was in
full session with no vacant seats, so Ling and I went into the dining
room for the usual dinner of Chinese chicken, the skin of which was
invariably black. Why an inscrutable Providence has granted the
people of China yellow skins and their chickens black is a subject
I should like to explore.

The Hostel was a cheap structure of wood and plaster with a small
amount of brick, originally built as a hospital. When foreigners began
to flock to Chungking, the government converted it into a hotel with
living quarters for foreigners only but with dining service open to all.
There was a large lounge with radio and stove, a spacious bare dining room, a few rooms for private parties, and a number of unheated
bedrooms. As at the *Café de la Paix* in Paris, foreign advisors, correspondents, businessmen, diplomats, as well as spies, crooks, whores,

and expatriates, wandered in and out. They came to eat foreign chow, such as it was, to sip tea or a drink, to play a game of bridge or poker, to flirt, or merely to drift about because of sheer ennui.

Ling had long ago thrown away his dictionary, and practiced poker diligently, dealing out imaginary hands at every opportunity. I had taught him the games I had learned at Monty's, as well as low ball, and had, only a few days earlier, written out instructions on the play of seven-card stud and had gone over these with him.

The instructions read:

SEVEN-CARD STUD

You are dealt three cards, two down and one up. Stay on the first three cards if you hold:

(1) Any three of a kind, and draw the limit, that is, the 4th, 5th, 6th and 7th cards.
(2) Two Aces or Two Kings, and draw the limit.
(3) Two Queens or less, and draw only *one* card and no more unless the hand is improved. The odds for making a winning hand are made prohibitive by drawing more cards.
(4) Any pair *with the Ace or King,* and draw *one* card and no more unless the hand is improved.
(5) Any 3-card straight or any 3-card flush, and draw only *two cards* and no more unless the hand is improved. If in five cards you make a 4-card flush or a 4-card straight, draw the 6th and 7th card.

Ling studied my instructions for a day or so and then came back with some questions.

"Advisor," he said, "I understand point one and two you make. But point three I do not understand. If you hold two queens, you say draw only one card unless the hand is improved. Why?"

"Because after the fourth card the betting gets too stiff even at limit poker (everything is relative you know), and the odds do not favor taking more cards. Of course if you make three of a kind, you go all the way. Suppose after the third card you hold Q Q 7, and draw a 9, making Q Q 7 9. The hand hasn't been improved and I recommend folding. The odds are against making three queens. Suppose you *do* draw a nine on the fifth card, making Q Q 7 9 9. That is queens up. I know from both experience and mathematics that queens up is not a winning hand."

"If I make queens up on the fifth card," said Ling "I may draw a nine or a Q on the sixth or seventh card and make a full house."

"You might," I agreed skeptically, "but it is roughly five to one you don't."

Ling wrote this on the page of instructions I had given him. "I don't understand point number four," he said. "What are you trying to make."

"Aces up or kings up or possibly three of a kind."

"Oh, I see," he said. "Now point five, how about that? Why draw only the fourth and fifth cards?"

"You know better than to ask that damn-fool question," I said. "Suppose you hold only a three-card straight or a three-card flush after the fifth card—you have to draw two of the same sequences in the case of the straight, or two of the same suit on the sixth and seventh cards to make the hand. The odds are prohibitive.

"Seven-card stud," I told Ling, "is more difficult than other games such as five-card stud, seven-card low stud, draw, and the like, because most players go for everything in the deck: straight flushes, fours, full houses, straights, flushes, three of a kind, two pairs and pairs. This means you need to watch your hands more closely, but once the rudiments are mastered, the game settles down to a routine, which gives you time to study your opponent's idiosyncrasies.

"I know one player," I told him, "who after the deal, when his time comes to bet, leans over and apparently studies one hand at a time. When he puts on this act he always bets or raises and it is a sure thing he has a strong hand. Another will light a cigarette and pretend not to know when his turn comes to bet; then after glancing around the tables, he bets. He has them. Another obvious case is the man who can't control his hands when going for a big pot. He probably made his hand as early as the fifth card and starts to shake before the end. Then there is the conversational player. 'Well, now,' he says, 'you made two aces on your fourth card. Maybe you made three of them. Did you? Well, just for that I'm going to make you a little bet.' Raise him. He's already lost his string. Another drums on the table with his fingers after a card hits him or after the draw in draw poker. Still another, who finds deception impossible, will beam at you when his hand is improved, and his face lights up like Broadway at night. Many players have trouble controlling their voices when they check, call or bet. A player who has a sensitive ear can detect this slight inflection of voice and read what it means. Still another, when his hand is improved, chokes up and can scarcely talk.

"If we set a specific limit," I went on, "we can determine the cost of the first three cards, two down and one up. Dollar limit is one of the most popular limits in which the dealer edges twenty-five cents. It follows that in seven-handed the player deals every seventh hand and for each round the cost to him will be twenty-five cents. In addition to edging every seventh hand, each player on the average will hold the high card (five- or seven-card stud) or the low card (seven-card low stud) which forces him to bet whether he wants to or not. One complete round of deals will therefore cost him fifty cents on the average if he bets twenty-five cents when he is forced to. He will receive seven hands of three cards each for fifty cents or an average of seven cents each. If it costs only seven cents to look at three cards it follows that the player may look at several hands before the cost becomes prohibitive. (Where the limit is larger or smaller these figures may be adjusted accordingly.)

"In this particular game, the player will get a hand which at least equals my minimum requirements to stay on, one time in seven. It will therefore cost the player forty-nine cents on the average to stay and take more cards. In most of the other poker games the staying requirements are such that you will stay in twice the number of pots, so the cost will be much less.

"To repeat," I said, "you will on the average play one hand in seven and win forty per cent of the hands played. The reason your winning average is so high is because you stay on strong hands only.

"Of course there will be a poor run of cards and a good run of cards but in six sittings of four hours each you will win five and lose once. But when you do lose, your losses should not be more than one-half of your average winnings per sitting.

"You should increase your winnings and lessen the losses by learning when to call and when to bluff. But whether you become proficient or not in the art of deceit, if you will only follow the minimum requirements to stay on you will come out winner. Remember it costs only seven cents to look at three cards. With the cost so small, why get involved on a weak hand? There is always another deal coming up.

"You must be more patient," I told Ling, "in seven-card stud, because I have restricted what you play on so drastically. But the pots are larger and you will win more, though not so often. The important thing is to avoid coming up with second-best hand. Be patient. Just stay in the deep freeze a bit longer."

A servant came in to tell us there was one vacant seat at the poker table. They played in one of the private rooms on the first floor on a large kitchen table. Ling and I had played there before, but I never ceased to marvel at the casual method of play. I had heard this is accepted style in the Orient, and if so, the card sharps had overlooked a lucrative field. To be sure it takes a lot of Chinese dollars to buy anything and the stakes were in Chinese money—bundles of it. The play was slovenly. No one paid attention to the rules as I know them and they often made new ones on the spot to cover a disagreement. With childish wishful thinking they disregarded all mathematical probabilities; they bet Chinese and Hong Kong money as if it had no value whatsoever, though to get it they must convert gold into Chinese or Hong Kong.

And, to my horror, they more often than not threw in their discards face up! They broke all the precepts on how to win at poker as known in my youth. Monty, in whose poker place I had cut my eye-teeth, would simply have passed out at the prospect of such an easy game as was afforded by the Hostel.

When I entered with Ling, the table was still full. Pop Weiner greeted me with, "I'm quitting in a moment, Osborn." He owned a compound along the North River, which flows into the Yangtze. Though a Dane, he claimed German citizenship since there was no Danish Government representative in Chungking to protect him. He was about seventy-five, sported a Kaiser mustache together with a Vandyke beard, and had lived in Chungking for forty-five years. He served tiffin to a nondescript lot of Chinese and foreigners, rented rooms to couples with no questions asked, and ran a bawdy house on the side. His specialty was Chinese college girls in distress, though if the truth were known they were prostitutes who had never seen the inside of a school except perhaps the "School for Scandal." Foreigners, especially the embassy crowd, fell for this coquettish masquerade. It was nothing to see a diplomat sneaking down the back stairs when he thought the coast was clear, hoping thus to be unseen lest he lose face in diplomatic society, such as it was.

Next to Pop sat a foreign code clerk, snobbish and curly-headed, who declaimed endlessly about going back to fight but did nothing about it. He had lost heavily to me on several occasions and for some reason seemed to make a personal issue out of this and was always baiting me.

Among the other five, I vaguely knew Herr Neilson, the antiaircraft advisor; a munitions salesman; two sailors from the gunboat; and a dizzy aviator who was in Chungking demonstrating pursuit planes. The next day I heard he had failed to come out of a nose dive, and he and his plane had disappeared into the muddy banks of the Yangtze.

The kibitzers were Ted White, a good-natured reporter from *Time* Magazine who hoped to write a book (and did, two best sellers, *Thunder Over China* and *Fire in the Ashes*); Bing, a boyish Chinese lad, foreign-dressed, suave and diplomatic, who Ling said was in our service spying on foreigners; a pleasant Irishman and a quarrelsome Britisher both having something to do with Chinese salt taxes. Most of them, including the advisors, were overpaid and attempted to get rid of their money at the poker table.

Also looking on was a striking black-haired woman. More than plump, she was smoking a huge black cigar. I had never seen her before, but when the men gathered about her called her Mickey, I knew she must be Miss Emily Hahn who, gossip said, was in Chungking to write the history of the three Soong sisters, Mmes Chiang, Kung, and Sun.

I pinched Ling's arm and nodded at the kibitzers. "What do you think?" I whispered.

He whispered back, "Old Chinese saying, 'When No Tiger in Mountain Then Monkey Is King.' "

I think Miss Hahn must have overheard for she wrote some uncomplimentary things about me in her book *China to Me* to which I will refer later.

Pop got up at last and gave me his seat, while Ling remained standing. They were playing the usual table stakes with dealer's choice— seven-card stud, Hi-Lo, stud, draw, spit-in-the-ocean and the like.

The code clerk, who held a job I had graduated from at half his age, had, as I said, taken an intense dislike to me and when I stayed in the pot bet in an attempt to run me out. Finally in seven-card stud, I made a straight on the fifth card—the first two were concealed— ? ? 9 10 J, and he showed three diamonds exposed: ? ? 9 6 Q
$$\diamond \diamond \diamond.$$
If the concealed cards were diamonds he held a flush which would beat my straight. But he was high with the queen, and checked. I bet 1,000 Chinese.

The next card I drew a 4, making ? ? 9 10 J 4, and he drew another diamond: ? ? 9 6 Q A
$$\diamond \diamond \diamond \diamond.$$
He was a plunger, and I knew would have bet the three diamonds, as he was optimistic enough to believe he would draw the fifth, had he had one in the hole, but now he had four diamonds exposed. He bet 2,000 Chinese just as if he had made his flush. Of course I could not improve my hand, having made a straight on the fifth card. Sound deduction told me he had not yet made the flush but hoped to do so on the seventh card. I raised him 2,000 Chinese and he just called.

Now I was sure. Had he made the flush he would have raised me back.

I had been counting the diamonds. Most persons successful in cryptography have what is known as a photographic mind; otherwise they could not retain in their minds the long sequences of code words and letters which must be remembered if the cipher is to be unraveled. This is not memory; it is mental photography. Without effort I could name every diamond that had been dealt.

Four had been dealt to the code clerk.

I held the seven and eight of diamonds in my own hand, unexposed. That made six.

On the first round, after the third card was dealt exposed, there were three more diamonds. That made nine.

On the next round two diamonds were exposed. That made eleven.

And on still the next round, the sixth, the twelfth diamond had been exposed.

That accounted for twelve diamonds.

If I had counted correctly there were now exactly fifteen cards in the pack. That made twenty-five cards which had not been exposed, excluding the code clerk's two hole cards. Among these there was only *one* diamond. Therefore, it was twenty-four to one the code clerk would not make his flush unless, of course, he had already made it—which was most unlikely.

He was dealing and dealt each of us a card, face down. The exposed ace of diamonds was still high and it was his bet. He still had some money in front of him. He emptied his pockets of Chinese, Hong Kong, and American money and counted it all out and threw it in the pot.

"How much is it?" I asked.

"About five thousand Chinese. Too much?" he sneered.

"Would any of your friends like to back your hand further?" I asked, looking at the kibitzers. When no one answered I said, "Not too much if you didn't make the fifth diamond. And I don't think you did. There's only one diamond left, and unless you have a horseshoe concealed somewhere, you didn't catch it."

I began to count out a bundle of Chinese dollars. "I call," I said and threw the money on the table. I spread my hand, revealing a jack high straight, 7 8 9 10 J.

Because of his insolence I dragged in the money even before he turned his hole cards.

"I'll play with you no more!" he cried, flushed and shaking, tearing up his cards. Then he paused and, to make his words more dramatic, curled his lips and sneered, "Major Herbert Osborn *Yardley*?"

He waited for something to happen, but no one so much as cracked a smile at the disclosure of my identity.

"Let's get out of here, Mickey," he said and left with Miss Hahn, who was entirely unperturbed and still puffing at her big black cigar.

I picked up the money to go.

"Bloody ass," said Bing. "Pay no attention. Sit down and play, Osborn."

"See you some other time," I said, a bit conscience-stricken, for I had taken some of their money too, and after the custom of the Orient they had all been decent enough not to inquire about me in public.

When we returned to the chateau the guard informed Ling that the Donkey was looking for us.

"What's up?" I asked.

Ling didn't know, but when the Donkey came in a few minutes later he seemed in quite a huff. He showed Ling a long cable from America, written in both Chinese and English. Ling handed me the English version which read, "Excerpts from the New York *Tribune* with a Shanghai date line."

So it was. I had been expecting something like this for some time, for sooner or later the correspondents would find out about me. The code clerk's disclosure was the forerunner. Now, judging from the Donkey's demeanor, I was in for it.

I do not have the exact words but the dispatch read something like this,

SHANGHAI. Information has leaked out of China that Major Herbert O. Yardley of Black Chamber fame is in Chungking unraveling Japanese code messages. Codeman Yardley, it is said, is working for the Generalissimo under an assumed name.

The dispatch shifted to Washington and continued,

The Department of State, when interviewed, declared that Yardley applied for a passport to travel in the British Empire as an importer. They denied knowledge of his present whereabouts.

Ted White in *Fire in the Ashes* has something to say about my activities:

"The sixth [meaning the author] was a balding middle-aged little fellow with the attractive and happy garrulousness of a country storekeeper. He purported to be a merchant of skins and hides and was the first American secret agent I ever met. His special skill was in cracking Japanese radio codes, and our Government had lent him to the Chinese Government to work on their intercepts of Japanese messages. He was an extremely witty man. At that time, we were not yet at war with Japan and therefore the embassy and all the embassy officials studiously avoided him, for, although half the gossipy town knew all about him, his mission was supposed to be ultrasecret. When old 'Osborn'—which was the name he used —talked of his boyhood in an Indiana town, in the sunlit days of the early century, or told the adventures of his bearded grandfather who was a Union veteran and the town drunk, it seemed wonderfully adventurous to all of us that he should now be here in the mysterious Orient cracking Japanese radio codes for Chiang Kaishek."

When I returned the cablegram to Ling, the Donkey looked at me angrily.

"What of it?" I said to Ling. "I've always told you my presence was no more than a Chinese secret. Tell the General that everyone here knows who I am."

"How?" asked the General.

"Well," I said, "to enumerate a few cases, since I have been here I have had five guards, two chauffeurs, two houseboys, one washamah and two cooks. Servants gossip."

"The General says the servants would never dare to gossip."

"Someone at the chateau stole my typewriter, some of my papers including my passport in the name of Yardley, and all of Ling's clothes. I suppose the thief won't talk for pay!" I said sarcastically.

"The General says the thief was one of the house servants who was caught and executed and your and Ling's effects were returned."

I was resolved not to be out-argued in this foolish dispute.

"Direct the General's attention to the Headquarters sign in Chinese on my car and the fact that my chauffeur is usually in uniform."

"The General says that no one knows what the sign says."

"It is the same sign all Chinese generals use in the streets," I remarked acidly.

The Donkey digested this and started on a new tack.

"The General thinks you associate too much with foreigners," Ling translated.

Having argued this subject often I refused to be drawn again and the Donkey talked on.

"He says this dispatch was written by a foreigner, and how could a foreigner know if you didn't tell him."

"Correspondents come and go," I said. "A newspaper thinks I am in Chungking. Several persons in America know I am, for I write to them. So for verification a correspondent need only look for a bald-headed man with his second finger on the right hand missing."

I had struck the right note at last. The Donkey was clearly impressed and went into a long conversation with Ling.

"The General suggests," Ling said gravely, "that the Advisor wear an artificial finger to prevent identification."

"What?" I said. "No wig?"

"He hasn't thought of that yet."

"Let's finish with this foolishness," I said. "Surely he realizes that since my identity has been officially verified it's too late for concealment."

The Donkey was mollified. A bald head and a missing finger rather than any carelessness or negligence on the part of the Chinese had led to my identification. The Donkey will sit up half the night, I thought, elaborating the point in an official document to his superiors. Perhaps he will make copies of this for various bureaus, and one for his own file. All officialdom becomes involved in red tape and suffocates under its own documents, but the Chinese, without the aid of dictaphones, duplicating machines, and other devices, are peculiarly lost in their own memoranda. They must be years and decades in arrears of events. One can visualize the governmental departments of the future steadily losing ground until eventually the morning memorandum on the desk of an executive will have to do with events which occurred in his grandfather's time and the Chinese ideal of identification of the living with their dead ancestors be wholly realized.

2.

The chateau had sustained a direct hit, killing a few tens of servants and guards, as Ling would put it. The chauffeur had taken Ling and me out the Chengtu road. The students had hidden in an old Buddhist cave. So it was that we moved to an apartment high up the promontory at the confluence of the North and Yangtze rivers. The offices occupied the caves below the apartment.

The Donkey and his radio-intercepting operators took the first and second floors, while I was given the third. I at last had a tiled bath with four bedrooms and a large living room with three charcoal fireplaces. The kitchen and servants' quarters were on the top floor. My suite of apartments had a private entrance which opened on the street.

"This is an opportunity," I told Ling, "to get rid of those five guards."

"The Service pays them," he had said. "What do you care?"

"I care a lot. I have to tip them every month, and getting kowtowed to when I come and go isn't worth the money."

"Not every foreigner is kowtowed to," Ling returned. "You are Honorable Advisor," he said slyly.

"Not every foreigner pays for it either," I grumbled.

The next day I came home alone and found Hugh Gibbs, my American embassy friend, who had turned on my gramophone and was dancing with a Chinese girl.

"What goes on at the embassy?" I asked.

"Oh, the usual horse and bull. Near bomb hits on the embassy here, destruction of missionary property, a few deaths. That sort of thing. You know the crowd."

"Maybe a little fun might help." I looked at his companion. "Chinese girl, for instance."

"Lose face," he said.

"No women at the embassy?" I asked. "What do they do for women?"

"They don't. They stay at home and practice the embassy's indoor sport. That reminds me," he laughed, "the Chinese have a word for it—'naughty.' "

"Naughty in Chinese is *Wan Pi*," I said.

"Sure, *Wan Pi*, play skin. Even girls say '*Ni shih wan pi,*' you is naughty."

"I'll leave you two in a moment and let you play any way you want. By the way, you remember Marguerite, the young Chinese girl who was teaching me Chinese. She's in Chengtu visiting friends but will be back in a month or so. I want to ask you something about her. You are a Chinese scholar. One night I helped her down these dark stairs to the street and we stood talking a moment. There were ricksha coolies sprawled on the sidewalk around the entrance and they laughed and said something that made her tremble. What could it have been?"

He laughed gustily. "Well, Osborn, you sure are naïve. They said, '*Yang-kueb tse ti kuei-t'ou pi chiao wu-men chungkuo-jen-ti ta ma?*' "

"You're a big help. What does it mean?"

He said, "It means something like this: 'Do Foreign Devils have bigger turtle-heads than we Chinese boys?' "

"Jesus," I said, "no wonder she trembled."

He kissed his companion, and as I left I saw her, Chinese fashion, wiping her mouth.

3. *Summary of Seven-Card Stud*

This will teach you to win at seven-card stud whether at limit poker or table stakes. What to stay on will be found on page 82.

THE PLAY

I have dealt three hands as exercises.

1ST DEAL

The Deal

				Two Down	One Up	
1st player is dealt				9 A	A	Two Aces.
2nd	"	"	"	7 8	9	3-Card Straight.
3rd	"	"	"	K K	J	Two Kings Concealed.
4th	"	"	"	a bust.		
5th	"	"	"	7 2	2	Two Deuces.
6th	"	"	"	a bust.		
7th	"	"	"	A K	8	Ace-King High.

The Betting

1st player is High with the Ace. He must bet.
2nd stays on a 3-Card Straight.
3rd stays on Two Concealed Kings.
4th folds on a bust.
5th makes a bad call and stays with Two Concealed Deuces.
6th and 7th fold.

The Deal

					Two Down	Two Up	
1st player is dealt a Q, making					9 A	A Q	Two Aces, no improvement.
2nd	"	"	"	" 3,	"	7 8	9 3	Did not improve.
3rd	"	"	"	" 7,	"	K K	J 7	Did not improve Two Kings.
5th	"	"	"	" 9,	"	7 2	2 9	Did not improve the Two Deuces.

The Betting

1st player is High with the Ace. He bets on Two Aces.
2nd calls with a 3-Card Straight.

1st Deal (*Continued*)

3rd calls with Two Kings, thinking 1st may have Two Aces.

5th calls with Two Deuces. I would personally throw this hand in the discards. The betting gets stiffer and since he did not improve the hand he should fold. In fact he should not have stayed in the first place.

The Deal

	Two Down	Three Up	
1st player is dealt a J, making	9 A	A Q J	Did not improve Two Aces.
2nd " " " " 6, "	7 8	9 3 6	A 4-Card Straight. He still has two cards to make his hand.
3rd " " " " 7, "	K K	J 7 7	Kings Up.
5th " " " " 6, "	7 2	2 9 6	Still Two Deuces. He has gone too far but suckers never learn and will take the 6th card.

The Betting

It is 3rd player's bet with Two Sevens exposed. He bets on Kings Up. 5th player is still trying to make Three Deuces and stays.

1st player calls on Two Aces.

2nd also calls on a 4-Card Straight.

The Deal

	Two Down	Four Up	
1st player is dealt a J, making	9 A	A Q J J	Aces Up.
2nd " " " " 3, "	7 8	9 3 6 3	Still a 4-Card Straight.
3rd " " " " 2, "	K K	J 7 7 2	Still Kings Up.
5th " " " an 8, "	7 2	2 9 6 8	Two Deuces or a 4-Card Straight.

The Betting

1st hand is high with Two Jacks. He bets on Aces Up.

2nd calls on a 4-Card Straight.

3rd calls on Kings Up.

5th calls on a 4-Card Straight.

The Deal

	Two Down	Four Up	One Down	
1st player is dealt a 10, making	9 A	A Q J J	10	Aces Up.
2nd " " " an A, "	7 8	9 3 6 3	A	A busted Straight.
3rd " " " a 5, "	K K	J 7 7 2	5	Kings Up.
5th " " " " 9, "	7 2	2 9 6 8	9	Nines Up.

The Betting

1st player looks like he may have a Straight. He bets on Aces Up.

2nd folds a busted Straight.

1st Deal (*Continued*)

3rd calls with Kings Up. A very poor call.
5th folds on Nines Up.

Winning Hand

Aces Up, held by 1st player.

2nd Deal

The Deal

	Two Down	One Up	
1st player is dealt	2 3	4	3-Card Straight.
2nd " " "	Q Q	6	Two Queens, Concealed
3rd " " "	4 4	7	Two Fours, Concealed.
4th " " "	a bust.		
5th " " "	" "		
6th " " "	A K	9	Ace-King High.
7th " " "	2 A	A	Two Aces, Concealed

The Betting

7th player is High with the Ace exposed. He bets.
1st calls on a 3-Card Straight.
2nd raises on Two Queens. He would have to make Three Queens or a Full House
    to hold a winning hand. Queens Up is a weak hand in Seven-Card Stud.
3rd stays on Two Fours. He should not have stood the raise.
4th and 5th hold busts and fold.
6th folds.
7th, with Two Aces, just calls. He thinks 2nd hand may have Three Sixes.
1st calls.

The Deal

	Two Down	Two Up	
1st player is dealt a 5, making	2 3	4 5	4-Card Straight.
2nd " " " " 7, "	Q Q	6 7	Did not improve Two Queens.
3rd " " " " 7, "	4 4	7 7	Sevens Up.
7th " " " " J, "	2 A	A J	Still Two Aces.

The Betting

3rd hand has Two Sevens Exposed and bets his Sevens Up. This is no hand to
    bet on. If he doesn't make a Full House, and the odds say he won't,
    he will most surely lose.
7th calls on Two Aces.
1st calls with a 4-Card Straight.
2nd calls with Two Queens—a poor call.

2ND DEAL (*Continued*)

The Deal

		Two Down	Three Up	

1st player is dealt a 6, making 2 3   4 5 6   He made the hand—a Six High Straight.

2nd "   "   "   " 6,   "   Q Q   6 7 6   Queens Up.

3rd "   "   "   " K,   "   4 4   7 7 K   Sevens Up. No change.

7th "   "   "   " J,   "   2 A   A J J   Aces Up. He improved.

The Betting

7th hand is High with Two Jacks Exposed. He bets, disregarding 1st hand's possible Straight.

1st player raises on a Six High Straight.

2nd foolishly calls, on Queens Up. Queens Up seldom win. He needs to make a Full House.

3rd is sucked in and also calls.

7th calls with Aces Up.

The Deal

		Two Down	Four Up	

1st player is dealt a 10, making 2 3   4 5 6 10   Six High Straight.

2nd "   "   "   " 10,   "   Q Q   6 7 6 10   Queens Up, no change.

3rd "   "   "   " J,   "   4 4   7 7 K J   Sevens Up, no change.

7th "   "   "   " 3,   "   2 A   A J J 3   Aces Up, no change.

The Betting

7th hand is High with Two Jacks exposed. He checks, fearing a Straight is held by 1st player.

1st bets on a Six High Straight.

2nd calls on Queens Up. He has lost all hope of winning unless he fills but it is about 11 to 1 he doesn't.

3rd calls on Sevens Up. He's in the same trap.

7th also calls. He's sure he has to fill to win with heavy odds against him.

The Deal

		Two Down	Four Up	One Down	

1st player is dealt a J, making 2 3   4 5 6 10   J   Six High Straight.

2nd "   "   "   " 4,   "   Q Q   6 7 6 10   4   Queens Up, no change.

3rd "   "   "   " 3,   "   4 4   7 7 K J   3   Sevens Up, no change.

7th "   "   "   " 9,   "   2 A   A J J 3   9   Aces Up, no change.

The Betting

7th player is still High with two exposed Jacks. He checks.

With 7th player checking, unless he's checking a cinch, 1st player has only 2nd and 3rd players to deal with. He suspects that each of them has been drawing to two pair. If he is a mathematician he knows it is about 5 to 1 that neither one made a Full House. He bets.

2ND DEAL (*Continued*)

2nd player is like so many card addicts he will call on anything. He calls.
3rd player is even worse than the 2nd player. He calls on Sevens Up, a hopeless call.
7th player with Aces Up has some reason for calling. He has a strong hand that will win most of the pots. But he should have observed the 1st player more closely. He started betting the moment he made his Straight.

Winning Hand
Small Straight, held by 1st player.

3RD DEAL

The Deal

	Two Down	One Up	
1st player is dealt	J J	J	Three Jacks Concealed.
2nd " " "	9 9	8	Two Nines Concealed.
3rd " " "	a bust.		
4th " " "	K Q	7	King-Queen High.
5th " " "	Q Q	7	Two Queens Concealed.
6th " " "	a bust.		
7th " " "	A 2	2	Two Deuces with the Ace.

The Betting
1st player is High with the Jack. He bets his Three Jacks.
2nd calls on Two Nines.
3rd folds with a bust.
4th calls on King High. This is a very poor call. Never call without holding a pair, a 3-Card Straight or flush.
5th hand raises with Two Queens. Very poor strategy.
6th folds with a bust.
7th calls with Two Deuces and the Ace. I would have folded after the raise.

1st hand does not wish to disclose his Three Jacks until the betting gets higher. He just calls.
2nd makes a bad call with Two Nines. A sucker play.
4th folds.

The Deal

		Two Down	Two Up	
1st player is dealt a	A, making	J J	J A	Still Three Jacks.
2nd " " " "	4, "	9 9	8 4	Still Two Nines.
5th " " " "	A, "	Q Q	2 A	Still Two Queens.
7th " " " "	A, "	A 2	2 A	Aces Up.

The Betting
1st player is still High with the Ace-Jack. He bets his Three Jacks.
2nd calls on Two Nines. An expensive call.

3RD DEAL (*Continued*)

5th calls on Two Queens.
7th raises on Aces Up.

1st player still does not wish to tip his hand. He just calls on Three Jacks.
2nd player is in a trap. But he calls.
5th is also trapped but calls.

The Deal

	Two Down	Three Up	
1st player is dealt a 6, making	J J	J A 6	Still Three Jacks.
2nd " " " " 3, "	9 9	8 4 3	Still Two Nines.
5th " " " " K, "	Q Q	2 A K	Two Queens.
7th " " " " 9, "	A 2	2 A 9	Aces Up.

The Betting

The 5th hand is High with Ace-King. He checks.
7th hand bets with Aces Up.

1st player has laid back long enough. He raises on Three Jacks.
2nd player has had enough and folds.
5th hand throws up the sponge.
7th player stays on Aces Up.

The Deal

	Two Down	Four Up	
1st player is dealt a 6, making	J J	J A 6 6	Jack Full. He improved.
7th " " " " 2, "	A 2	2 A 9 2	Deuce Full. He improved.

The Betting

1st player bets with a Jack Full.
7th raises on a Deuce Full.

1st raises.
2nd calls.

The Deal

	Two Down	Four Up	One Up	
1st player is dealt a 10, making	J J	J A 6 6	10	Jack Full.
2nd " " " " 10, "	A 2	2 A 9 2	10	Deuce Full.

The Betting

1st player is still High with the Ace-Jack. He bets on the Jack Full.
2nd player calls.

Winning Hand

Jack Full, held by 1st player.

III

Seven-Card Stud (Hi-Lo)

———◆————————————————————————————————

Summary of Hi-Lo will be found on pages 100-107. This will teach you to win whether at limited poker or at table stakes.

1.

I had earlier given Ling a treatise on seven-card stud, Hi-Lo, which he had studied. It read:

LOW

In Seven-Card Stud, Hi-Lo, A 2 3 4 5, unlike Seven-Card Low Stud, is a straight or a flush. A 2 3 4 6 is the *lowest* hand in this game. Low winning hands are quoted below. None of them are straights.

Lowest Hand
A 2 3 4 6

6 Low
A 2 3 5 6
A 2 4 5 6
A 3 4 5 6

7 Low

A 2 3 4 7
A 2 3 5 7
A 2 4 5 7
A 3 4 5 7
A 2 3 6 7
A 3 4 6 7
2 3 4 6 7
A 3 5 6 7
2 3 5 6 7
A 4 5 6 7

All cards which are *below* an eight, A 2 3 4 5 6 7, I call the Winning Zone. All others, 8 9 10 J Q K, I call the Losing Zone. You are dealt Two Down and One Up in Hi-Lo. If all three are in the Winning Zone, raise. *Example 1*: A 5 7

If two cards are in the Winning Zone and one in the Losing Zone, just call. *Example 2*: A 7 K

If only one card is in the Winning Zone and two in the Losing Zone, fold. *Example 3*: A J K

If all three cards are in the Losing Zone, fold. *Example 4*: 8 J Q

What you are trying to get for Lo are five cards out of seven in the Winning Zone; that is, five cards below an eight.

In *Example 1*, A 5 7: If you draw another in the Winning Zone, A 5 7 4, then bet because you have four out of five in the Winning Zone. If the fifth card is also in the Winning Zone, of course you continue to bet.

If in *Example 1*, A 5 7, you draw the fourth card in the Losing Zone, you can still make a low hand: A 5 7 K.

If you draw the fifth card in the Losing Zone, A 5 7 K J, your chances are not so good, but stay for another card.

If the sixth card is in the Losing Zone, A 5 7 K J Q, then fold because you have only one more card to draw and you can't possibly make a Low Hand.

Refer to *Example 2*, A 7 K. If you draw a card in the Winning Zone, A 7 K 3, then stay.

Suppose on the other hand the fourth card is in the Losing Zone, A 7 K J. You now have two in the Winning Zone and two in the Losing Zone. To make a Low hand you would have to draw three consecutive cards in the Winning Zone and the odds are prohibitive against your doing so. Fold. *Always fold with two in the Winning and two in the Losing Zone.*

Drawing a pair in the Winning Zone is the same as drawing a card in the Losing Zone. A 7 K J has the same value as A 7 7 K, or rather, it is even higher because you have a pair of Sevens for Lo.

HIGH

I ask you now to forget everything I have previously told you about Seven-Card High. This game has absolutely no relation to Hi in Hi-Lo. You don't stay on anything but the *highest* hands. In Hi, of Hi-Lo, go for Aces Up, Three of a Kind, Straights, Flushes, Full Houses. In Lo, as already directed, go for five cards ranging from Ace to Seven.

To repeat, for *High* STAY on

(1) Two Aces, such as A A 5. This is the ideal hand to go for both High and Low. A A K is not so good for Two are in the Losing Zone.

(2) Never stay on K K 10 or Q Q 7 or the like. It is too difficult to make Threes, and the pots are split. But stay with a pair if two cards are in the Winning Zone such as 2 2 7, 3 3 6, 4 4 5, and 5 5 7.

(3) Three of a Kind. This is a good hand and you may make a Full House, and occasionally Four of a Kind.

(4) Three of the same suit or three of the same sequence. You are trying to make a Flush or a Straight. But if the hand is not improved on the fourth card, fold. The betting gets too rough to draw more cards; also the pots are split, so the percentage for gain is lessened.

Stay on Hi-Lo hands which offer the best chances to win either Hi or Lo or both. Two deals follow which may be used as exercises.

TWO DEALS OF HI-LO

1st Deal

The Deal		*Two Down*	*One Up*	
1st player is dealt		2 3 ♣ ♣	7 ♣	Three clubs. He may make a flush for Hi hand. Also three in Winning Zone (see page 101, *Example 1*). He may make the Lo hand. In fact it is possible to make both a flush and Lo hand. This is one of the ideal hands to draw to.
2nd " " "		4 5	K	Two in Winning Zone, One in Losing Zone. Just call. (See also page 101, *Example 2*.)
3rd " " "		2 K	J	One in Winning Zone, Two in Losing Zone. Fold. (See also *Example 3*, page 101.)
4th " " "		8 10	Q	Three in Losing Zone. Fold. (See *Example 4*, page 101.)
5th " " "		2 2	Q	The Deuces are paired so Two are in Losing Zone. Fold. Do not play a small pair unless Two Cards are in the Winning Zone.
6th " " "		K K	9	Two Kings look like a good hand for Hi. It is difficult to make Three Kings. And if you make only Kings Up you will win only thirty per cent of the time, which is good enough but the pots are split, giving you only fifteen per cent.
7th " " "		8 9	10	A 3-Card Straight. Take only the 4th card and if you do not improve, fold.

1ST DEAL *(Continued)*

The Betting

> 2nd player is High with the King and must bet. He bets with Two cards in the Winning Zone.
>
> 3rd hand folds with Two in Losing Zone.
>
> 4th folds with Three in Losing Zone.
>
> 5th folds with only One in Winning Zone and Two in Losing Zone.
>
> 6th hand folds Two Kings.
>
> 7th calls with a 3-Card Straight.

> 1st player raises with Three Clubs in the Winning Zone. He may make Hi or Lo or both.
>
> 2nd hand calls with Two in Winning Zone.
>
> 7th calls with a 3-Card Straight.

The Deal

	Two Down	Two Up	
1st player is dealt an A, making	2 3 ♣	7 A ♣♣	Four Clubs, Four in Winning Zone. Bet because there is a good chance of making the Flush and five cards in Winning Zone.
2nd " " " a 7, "	4 5	K 7	Three in Winning Zone, One in Losing Zone. Bet because Two more cards in Winning Zone should give 2nd player a good hand.
7th " " " a J, "	8 9	10 J	A 4-Card Straight. If he had not improved he should have folded.

The Betting

> 1st player is High with the Ace. He bets on Four Clubs and Four in Winning Zone.
>
> 2nd calls with Three in Winning Zone, One in Losing Zone.
>
> 7th calls on a 4-Card Straight.

The Deal

	Two Down	Three Up	
1st player is dealt a 7, making	2 3 ♣♣	7 A 7 ♣♣♠	He paired. Still has Four Clubs and Four in Winning Zone.
2nd " " " an A, "	4 5	K 7 A	Four in Winning Zone, One in Losing Zone. He should bet with Four in Winning Zone and the sixth and seventh card to come.
7th " " " a Q, making	8 9	10 J Q	A Queen High Straight. He should raise.

1st Deal (*Continued*)

The Betting

1st player is high with Two Sevens. He bets with Four Clubs and Four in Winning Zone.

2nd player calls with Four in Winning Zone.

7th player raises with a Queen High Straight.

1st re-raises with Four Clubs and Four in Winning Zone.

2nd just calls with Four in Winning Zone.

7th timidly calls with Queen High Straight. He is afraid 1st player will catch a club on either the 6th or 7th card.

The Deal

	Two Down	Four Up	
1st player is dealt a 4, making	2 3 ♣	7 A 7 4 ♣♣ ♣♣♠♣	A 2 3 4 7 for Lo and Five Clubs for Hi. A raising hand.
2nd " " " a 3, "	4 5	K 7 A 3	A 3 4 5 7 for Lo—a raising hand.
7th " " " a 9, "	8 9	10 J Q 9	A Straight. A raising hand.

The Betting

1st player is High with Two Sevens. He bets on A 2 3 4 7 for Lo and a Flush for Hi.

2nd raises on A 3 4 5 7 for Lo.

7th hand calls on Queen High Straight.

1st player has one of the lowest hands in the deck—A 2 3 4 7 and a cinch for Hi. He re-raises.

2nd player also has a below average Lo hand but he just calls.

7th hand, from what he can see, thinks he has High hand but calls.

The Deal

	Two Down	Four Up	One Down	
1st player is dealt a 10, making	2 3 ♠	7 A 7 4 ♣♣ ♣♣♠♣	10 ♠	A Flush for Hi and A 2 3 4 7 for Lo. He may win both.
2nd " " " an 8, "	4 5	J 7 A 3	8	A 3 4 5 7 for Lo.
7th " " " a 10, "	8 9	10 J Q 9	10	Queen High Straight.

The Betting

1st player is High with Two Sevens. He bets on a Flush for Hi and A 2 3 4 7 for Lo.

2nd just calls on A 3 4 5 7 for Lo.

7th player calls.

Winning Hand

A 2 3 4 7 for Lo.

A Flush for Hi, both held by 1st player.

2ND DEAL

The Deal

			Two Down	One Up	
1st player is dealt			A A	5	Two Aces for Hi and Two in Winning Zone for Lo. See (1) and *Example 2*, page 101.
2nd	"	" "	4 5	7	Three in Winning Zone for Lo. *See Example 1*, page 101.
3rd	"	" "	7 8	10	One in Winning Zone, Two in Losing Zone for Lo. This hand should be folded. See *Example 3*, page 101.
4th	"	" "	Q Q	8	Two Queens for Hi. This player has a good chance for making Queens Up but it is a losing hand. See (2), page 102. In the *1st Deal* 6th player rightly folded Two Kings. This player will stay on a worse hand—Two Queens.
5th	"	" "	2 2	7	Two Deuces for Hi, and Two in Winning Zone for Lo. See latter part of (2), page 102.
6th	"	" "	9 9	9	Three Nines for Hi. A good hand. See (3), page 102.
7th	"	" "	J Q	K	Three in the same sequence for Hi. See (4), page 102.

The Betting

7th hand is Hi with the King. He bets on a 3-Card Straight.

1st player raises on Two Aces and Two in Winning Zone.

2nd stays on Three in Winning Zone.

3rd hand folds.

4th makes a bad call on Two Queens.

5th calls on Two Deuces and Two in Winning Zone.

6th hand raises on Three Nines.

7th calls on a 3-Card Straight.

1st calls on Two Aces and Two in Winning Zone.

2nd calls on Three in Winning Zone.

4th makes another bad call on Two Queens.

5th calls on Two Deuces and Two in Winning Zone.

The Deal

				Two Down		Two Up	
1st player is dealt a 10, making				A A		5 10	Two Aces for Hi and a bare possibility of Lo with Two in Winning Zone and Two in Losing Zone.
2nd	"	" "	" J,	"		4 5 7 J	Three in Winning Zone and One in Losing Zone for Lo.
4th	"	" "	" K,	"		Q Q 8 K	Still Two Queens for Hi.
5th	"	" "	" 3,	"		2 2 7 3	Two Deuces for Hi and Three in Winning Zone for Lo.
6th	"	" "	" 3,	"		9 9 9 3	Three Nines for Hi.
7th	"	" "	" 8,	"		J Q K 8	He did not improve on the 4th card and should fold.

2ND DEAL *(Continued)*

The Betting

4th player is Hi with K 8. He should not bet but does. In fact he should have
folded in the first place.

5th calls on Two Deuces for Hi and Three in Winning Zone for Lo.

6th raises on Three Nines for Hi.

7th did not improve on 4th card and should fold but he calls.

1st and 2nd hands call.

4th calls on Two Queens. He knows he is beat but is still stubborn.

5th calls on Two Deuces for Hi and Three in Winning Zone for Lo.

The Deal

	Two Down	Three Up	
1st player is dealt a 10, making	A A	5 10 10	Aces Up for Hi.
2nd " " " " 2, "	4 5	7 J 2	Four in Winning Zone, One in Losing Zone for Lo.
4th " " " " K, "	Q Q	8 K 4	No change.
5th " " " an A, "	2 2	7 3 A	Four in Winning Zone, One in Losing Zone for Lo.
6th " " " a J, "	9 9	9 3 J	Three Nines for Hi.
7th " " " " 4, "	J Q	K 8 4	Did not improve the Straight.

The Betting

1st player is Hi with Two Tens. He has Aces Up but is afraid of 6th player's
raise. He checks.

2nd hand has Four in Winning Zone and two more cards to make a low hand.
He bets.

4th folds.

5th with Four in Winning Zone and two more cards to come raises.

6th player with Three Nines for Hi raises.

7th with a 3-Card Straight folds.

1st player calls all bets with Aces Up.

2nd calls with Four in Winning Zone.

5th calls with Four in Winning Zone.

The Deal

	Two Down	Four Up	
1st player is dealt an 8, making	A A	5 10 10 8	Aces Up for Hi.
2nd " " " a K, "	4 5	7 J 2 K	Four in Winning Zone for Lo with one more card.
5th " " " " 5, "	2 2	7 3 A 5	A 2 3 5 7 for Lo, a very good hand.
6th " " " an 8, "	9 9	9 3 J 8	Three Nines for Hi.

The Betting

1st player checks on Aces Up for Hi. By now he should have figured 6th hand
for Three Nines.

2ND DEAL (*Continued*)

2nd player needs a card below a 7 for a Lo hand. He checks.

5th hand bets with A 2 3 5 7 for Lo.

6th hand is now confident he has the Hi hand and doesn't want other Hi hands drawing against him. He raises.

1st calls on Aces Up.

2nd calls.

5th re-raises on A 2 3 5 7 for Lo.

6th re-raises with Three Nines for Hi.

1st is in a trap and folds.

2nd folds.

5th player sees he will split the pot with 6th player and just calls. Both will go through the motions of taking the seventh card.

The Deal

	Two down	Four Up	One Down	
5th player is dealt an A, making	2 2	7 3 A 5	A—	A 2 3 5 7 for Lo.
6th " " " a 7, "	9 9	9 3 J 8	7—	Three Nines for Hi.

Winning Hand

A 2 3 5 7 for Lo held by 5th player.

Three Nines for Hi held by 6th player.

2.

The Donkey had flooded the city with his own spies, who carried around wireless direction finders concealed in sedan chairs in an attempt to find unauthorized sending stations. He had spoken to me about one such transmitter being in the German Consulate next to the Hostel, and by the way he looked at me intimated that a German girl I was running around with might be involved. I had met her at Pop Weiner's and when he was killed during a bombing raid had taken her to the German Consulate. Her maiden name was Maria Lohmann. She had married a Chinese in Germany, but when he brought her back to Chengtu he had reduced her status to that of concubine, taking his Number One concubine as wife. Maria had escaped to Chungking and planned to move on to Shanghai if she could raise the airplane fare.

Ling, Maria and I were on our way to the Hostel for a few drinks and a game of poker. It was early April and the coolie-farmers along the way had planted vegetables and were watering them with liquid human excrement and fighting swarms of malaria-laden mosquitoes.

The moon would be full tonight, I reflected, a good time for bombers. At the Hostel a game was about to begin. One of the players, whom we had seen before, was supposed to be a refugee who had fled Nazi tyranny in Germany. He was about thirty, a big blond, soft spoken, and he carried himself like a soldier. If his hair had once been cropped, he had let it grow. I had asked Ling to look him up. The file merely stated that he was a German refugee, carrying seven pieces of baggage from Hong Kong to Chungking, and that he was traveling on a Honduran passport—doubtless bought in Paris, I reflected.

We took the two seats that were open. The German sat at Ling's right and the sailor to my left. The other seats were occupied by the munitions salesman; a CNAC pilot; and Herr Neilson, the anti-aircraft advisor. The only kibitzers were Maria, Bing, who spied on foreigners, and a Polish girl who broadcast Chinese propaganda—for what reason I could never understand, but then most foreigners managed to get on the Chinese payroll. The game was slovenly, as usual, and it seemed to me the stakes were higher, though it might have been because the hands were bigger.

The game progressed as usual and I was beginning to get bored when suddenly the German bet 5,000 Chinese which at that time was $500 in United States currency. They were playing seven-card stud, Hi-Lo. Ling called, and the sailor said he was broke and would have to stay for just the pot. He was high with three kings exposed which looked like he would split the money in the pot, holding Hi. When the sailor said he was broke, the German put the money to one side, indicating his bet was a side bet. Ling called and placed his money beside the German's.

The German held ? ? 2 4 7 with two more cards to come. He was doubtless going for low and if he held two cards below the 7 in the hole he should have a winning hand.

Ling held ? ? 6 3 4, also with two more cards to come.

The German was dealing and he dealt Ling the deuce, making ? ? 6 3 4 2. He dealt himself the ace of diamonds, making ? ? 2 4 7 A. I think he dealt a queen to the sailor but he was going for high and I didn't notice. I was only interested in the low hands.

When the German caught the ace of diamonds on the sixth card, making ? ? 2 4 7 A, I thought I detected a certain agitation reflected in Ling's eyes. It might have meant that he was disturbed over the German having made a four-card low hand. If the German had a trey unexposed he would have A 2 3 4 7 for low—very, very low indeed. Of course Ling could have a lower hand if one of his unexposed cards was an ace—namely, A 2 3 4 6, the lowest hand in the deck.

Another possibility crossed my mind. I had seen Ling eying the exposed discards, making mental notes, I thought. He had a better photographic mind than I and if he had taken the trouble to remember the cards that were exposed, as I always did, he would know many sequences of cards—if the sequences had not been disturbed in the shuffle. The German shuffled overhand, which is no shuffle at all. Could it be that Ling knew, or thought he knew, the next card—the next one to the ace of diamonds? If it turned out to be another ace, Ling would make the lowest hand in the deck. But, if the dealer suddenly called for a cut, Ling would be lost.

"What's the Hong Kong rate of exchange?" asked the German in a low voice.

"About four Hong Kong to one U.S.," said the CNAC pilot.

"I bet one thousand U.S.," declared the German. "Here's two thousand Hong Kong, which is five hundred U.S., and here's another five hundred gold," he said, and taking a bulging wallet from his pocket he counted off five hundred-dollar bills in United States money.

Ling studied the situation intently for several moments. At last he counted out the money he had in front of him, then reached for his wallet. There was barely enough to call the $1,000 gold bet. Ling hasn't made the hand, I thought, for if he had he would have raised and borrowed from me.

The German dealt Ling, the sailor, and himself the seventh card, face down.

The German sat to the left of the sailor; it was his bet. He gave his hole card a superficial look. He must already have made his hand, I thought—A 2 3 4 7. He opened his huge wallet again and took out a sheaf of hundred-dollar United States bills. Counting out twenty of them, he threw them in as a side bet.

"I bet two thousand dollars gold," he said. His voice did not rise.

Ling had flipped back his seventh card and looked at me. I thought I saw a look of triumph in his eyes.

"Advisor," he said, "you got any money?"

I had just that day made a deposit at the Bank of China, and having lost several good hands, had scarcely any money in front of me.

"I have my escape money," I said, trying to laugh but making a poor job of it.

When Ling didn't ask again I unbuttoned the belt of my trousers and took off my money belt, opened the cloth guard and threw twenty one-hundred-dollar bills in the pot.

"You're called," said Ling.

"What have you got?" asked the German.

"I called," said Ling.

The German spread his hand. He held A 2 3 4 7.

Ling turned over the seventh card. It was the ace of spades. A 2 3 4 6 stared up at the German. "That wins," he said and with well-disciplined self-assurance arose from the table.

I hurried Maria and Ling to the car, trying not to appear disturbed. I put my fingers to my lips, indicating the chauffeur.

After returning to the apartment I said, "Let's look at that money, Ling." He pulled from his pockets the Chinese, Hong Kong and United States money he had gathered from the poker table. I arranged the United States money according to numbers. They began with E 048936642 Y and ended with E 048936965 Y.

"Christ," I said, "the serial numbers indicate the German had over 30,000 gold in his purse—that is, if the numbers run consecutively,"

"They do," declared Ling. "The first five bills he took from the left side of his wallet, the next twenty he took from the right."

"That's a hell of a lot of money for a refugee to be carrying around. Ling, he's no Jew," I said. "He's a squarehead Nazi agent."

I looked to Maria for confirmation. *"Das Schweinehund,"* she spat.

"Maria," I said, "your consulate is under suspicion of communication with the enemy by radio. I think, instead, the radio is in the Hostel." I went to my bedroom and got the radio direction finder I had brought with me, which was more accurate than those of the Service. I set it at 13 KCS, the position of the suspected radio. "I'll put this in a suitcase. Take it to your room in the consulate, turn on the switch, and put on the ear phones. If you hear signals, watch this hand. It will point toward the sending radio. You understand?"

She nodded dubiously.

"You want to get to Shanghai?" I asked.

"Oh, yes, more than anything else. It means I'll be reunited with my family in Germany."

"Then do as I say. Whether you are successful or not, I'll see that you get to Shanghai. Furthermore the Chinese Government will be grateful and will repay you. The car will wait for you. No matter what time of night it is, if you hear signals come back to tell us—and watch the little hand."

"Clean that money off the table before the servants see it," I told Ling after Maria had gone. He returned my $2,000 loan and I put it back in my money belt while he counted the rest like a miser. "Quite a haul," I said and poured two drinks of the Hatchet Man's best brandy.

His lips curled in a silly grin. "You think I play better than in Hong Kong?"

"You graduated with honors," I said gravely. "But you'd have been a sick cat if that last card hadn't been an ace."

"Chinese like to gamble," he said. "But as you say, the odds favored me. The ace of spades was next to the ace of diamonds. The German didn't shuffle the cards much."

Ling took a deck of cards from his pocket and began to deal to himself, while I lay stretched on the couch.

"Ling," I said, "wasn't your ass puckering a little before you caught that ace of spades?"

3.

Time dragged on and I fell asleep. Suddenly there was a commotion in the hall and Maria rushed in unannounced. I jumped from the couch. "Well?" I asked.

She was out of breath. "The little hand points at the Hostel."

"What time did you hear the signals?"

"At 12:15."

"How long did they transmit?"

"About five minutes."

"Here, take a drink of brandy. You need it."

"Prosit," she said, gulping it down.

"You have any trouble getting out?"

"No, I came down the back stairs."

"Advisor, what do we do now?" Ling asked.

"Keep the German under surveillance and move some of our good equipment up close to the Hostel and intercept his messages. If he has made contact with the enemy I want no one to bother him but let him continue to send and receive. His code will not be too difficult to break. When we have enough of it I think I can read it. He must be one of a group of agents and we want to catch the whole crowd. Let him become suspicious and we fail to break up the plot, whatever it is."

"The Donkey won't let a spy go free here. He'll capture him at the first chance and cut off his head."

"And thus destroy his usefulness to us," I said, none too hopeful that my plan would be followed.

We heard talking outside the apartment, followed by the tread of heavy shoes on the stairs. I opened the door to see a long file of soldiers led by the Donkey. The Donkey gave some command to the soldiers and, ignoring me, brushed in and spoke peremptorily to Ling in Chinese. Ling turned a sickly greenish yellow, like an unripe apple.

I turned to Maria. "We have a conference. Please go into the back bedroom and close the door."

As I started to protest the Donkey's summary action Ling said, "Keep your head, Advisor, or you'll lose it and mine and Maria's as well. The Donkey has come to arrest you and Maria."

"Go on," I said. "What else?"

"He says the wireless at the German compound is giving out signals and is being answered. Messages in both directions have been intercepted. You and Maria are being held for investigation."

"Here?"

"No, in prison. I've told him nothing. Think fast. You know prisons. Anything can happen in them."

The Donkey, eying me impatiently, spoke again to Ling.

"He wants to know if you have anything to say."

"No," I said, pouring myself another drink. "You go ahead and tell the whole story, how we suspected the German because he carried a big bundle of cash, how Maria took my direction finder to the German consulate and located the sender in the Hostel."

There ensued a long and animated discussion. Finally Ling turned to me.

"The Donkey says you and Maria are under house arrest. He will send men to the Hostel and arrest the German. He says if it is found that there is a wireless in his room the house arrest will be lifted."

Ling looked hopefully at me. He had, he seemed to imply, escaped the worst. But the Donkey's stupidity and his interference in my plans left me coldly furious.

"Did you explain to the dumb son-of-a-bitch that I wanted to wait, before making an arrest, to decipher the messages and catch the German's confederates?"

"Yes, I told him all that. But he is hungry like a bloodhound."

"Very well," I said, seeing that I was licked. "But tell him also that if the German is found guilty the Advisor, in justice to his honor, will go to Number One or in his absence to the Generalissimo himself, to report the insults which have been heaped on him."

As Ling talked I could see that the Donkey was torn between disbelief and fear that what I threatened might come true.

"The Donkey says," Ling translated, "that if he has been unjust he will be the first to apologize."

"Damned nice of him," I replied. "Just to make sure he doesn't double-cross me you are to go along with him."

Waiting for them to return I fell asleep again. "The Donkey has come," said Ling, awaking me after what seemed only a moment. There was no pounding on doors this time but a ceremonious announcement. I told Ling to show the Donkey in. The Donkey, standing in the doorway, bowed respectfully, and Ling grinned.

"The General offers his apologies," Ling translated. "The Honorable Advisor has displayed great skill and patriotism and the miserable German is already in prison and his radio seized. He swallowed his code and is awaiting trial."

It would be some trial, I thought, if the poor wretch was not indeed already dead.

Miss Emily Hahn in *China to Me* gives a good description of the arrest:

> In actuality he [meaning the author] was a secret agent and everyone knew his real name, and his reason for keeping the German mistress who hung around the Hostel. Once when we were suddenly caught by the blackout she was noticed by Morgan sneaking into the Hostel when we had all been ordered to stay out of doors. She must have crept up the steps during the raid and indulged in her nefarious trade in the room of a German soi-disant refugee. A few nights later the refugee was arrested by Chinese soldiers. It was just like a movie; the German protested he had nothing to hide, though they searched his rooms and found a transmitter there. He chewed up a paper and tried to swallow it. It had a code on it, *exactly* like the movies.

Everybody was badly shaken by the scene. Hitherto we had accepted him as a perfectly pukka refugee. He didn't seem surprised at the arrest, or even very indignant. He was angry and violent—he pulled a gun on the soldiers, and there was a struggle—but he wasn't surprised.

"Let me get dressed, will you?" he said. The soldiers let him dress, tied his hands with rope, and then marched him out past all of us, standing there in our pajamas in a row, our mouths hanging open. He didn't look at any of us. That was queer too. If it had been me I should have appealed to the crowd, but he didn't.

Next day several people at the Hostel were all for Taking Steps. There was an uneasy feeling that we Europeans should stick together, and that no doubt it was all a fantastic mistake. Suppose it was a mistake? Allegedly he had been tortured by the Nazis before he escaped from Europe. So how could he possibly have been a spy for the Axis?

Certain newspapermen, as usual, acted as if they knew all about it but weren't talking. The American secret agent certainly did know, but he isn't talking either. I wonder if he tells his friends the things he used to tell us while playing poker. I shouldn't think so. Most of his conversation in those days was about women, and everyone in the Hostel knew exactly what money he was giving the German lady, and for what specific purpose. He didn't talk about those visits upstairs during the blackouts, though.

Miss Hahn is under at least one illusion. If Maria was seen upstairs at the Hostel it was because she was going to the ladies' room.

I thought this an opportune time to get money for Maria's transportation to Shanghai and I went to the bedroom and awakened her.

I spoke to the Donkey. "Miss Lohmann has displayed great daring and skill. Ling has already told you of her exploits. At great danger she carried my direction finder to her room in the German compound and located the German sending in the Hostel. I told her she would be well paid for her services. She needs a ticket on the plane to Shanghai and a generous expense account. I hope you will provide handsomely for her."

The General nodded and spoke to his adjutant, and Maria followed him to the second floor after giving me a tearful farewell.

"I wish to question the prisoner," I said and we tramped out, guards and all. On the way to the prison we picked up the Service doctor. We acquainted him with the situation so he came well supplied with Sodium Amytal and, in lieu of a stomach pump, a Chinese drug which would make the prisoner throw up.

The German protested vehemently but the guards forced his mouth open and held his nose as the doctor poured some vile concoction down his throat. The prisoner retched repeatedly until at last among other assorted debris he threw up the paper. I examined it eagerly but the stomach acids had eaten away the writing and I had no equipment with which to restore it.

They had placed the poor devil in a cage with the scum of Chungking, who looked on curiously while he retched. Convulsed with stomach spasms, he held on to the steel bars of the cage. Finally he became quieter and sat on the stone floor, his head in his hands.

"Tell the Donkey," I told Ling, "that I want to talk to the prisoner alone." And the Donkey, eager now to placate me, consented. I had the prisoner placed on a bamboo cot and there let him rest. After a time he opened his sickly eyes.

"We are both white men in the Orient," I said. "Because you are a white man I will try to save your life, if you will tell me everything."

"I have nothing to tell," he said in a shaky voice. "Nearly all foreigners in China have radios." He licked his feverish lips. I called to the guard for a glass of tea and when the prisoner had drunk I told him to rest and lit a cigarette for him.

"Foreigners have receiving sets," I told him, "but not sending sets. I put a direction finder on you, and you were sending. As you know, that means death."

"It isn't true," he said weakly.

"It's true enough. But true or not, you'll lose your head if you don't come clean. You are traveling on a Honduran passport. You have no extraterritoriality. Just one more thing," I said. "I will learn the truth, however much you may deny it. I'm going to place you under Sodium Amytal, a drug which will force you to talk as it has all the others. I will learn all about you or much of it. You do not believe this, but nevertheless it's true. If under its influence you tell me what you tell me now, I will say you have confessed everything and should not be executed." As he continued to hesitate I added, "Guilty or innocent, you are already convicted. But—I repeat—because you are a white man and I am a white man I will try to save your life."

I had little sympathy for him. But in trying to save him I was thinking of other foreigners. The execution of a foreigner for spying would be known to every Chinese, high and low, and Chinese suspicion of foreigners, already great, would make life in China even more hazardous than it was. Mob violence against the "Foreign Devils" had been known before.

"I have nothing to lose, I see," the German said, his lips white. Then he proceeded to tell me he had been groomed for this mission with a fake escape against Nazi tyranny. He had bought a Honduran passport and was to contact one Sin Fu at the Japanese consulate in Hong Kong. He had been given $35,000 gold (and at this he smiled ruefully at me) and had been directed to come to Chungking and await the arrival of still another agent.

"What were you sending?"

"Merely contact signals. Nothing more."

"What was the code?"

"Two figure numerals in German. I don't remember it."

"What was the mission of the other agent?"

"I don't know exactly. He was to contact a man on the Generalissimo's staff and I was to pay him twenty-five thousand dollars gold in hundred-dollar bills."

"For what?"

"I don't know."

"You have an idea. Remember, I'm going to use the drug on you."

"Well, at the consulate I heard scraps of conversation about a map. I know some Japanese. They pointed out Ichang, which is about two hundred miles downstream on the map."

"Did you hear the word *assassinate* linked with any reference to the Generalissimo?"

"No, but I had the feeling that they were going to try to kidnap him by paratroopers."

The more I questioned him the more confused he got, so I decided to give him the drug, all the while cursing the Donkey for having shattered a plot in the making.

I called in Ling and the Donkey and reviewed the questions I had asked. Under Sodium Amytal the German repeated his story as he had told it before, but under questioning was even more convinced that the plan was to kidnap the Generalissimo. He was placed in a private cell and permitted to sleep.

Had I condemned him to a life of misery? Almost gladly I remembered that prisoners were not taken to dugouts during air raids. The Japanese bombers might effect the release I had denied him.

4.

The next morning when I awakened the sun was up. There was a shuffle of feet in the hall and Ling opened the door. "A foreign gentleman has come," he said.

It was an American military commissioner with a roving itinerary in the Orient. I had met him several times before when he was in town. In fact, when he felt the need of a Chinese girl he made himself at home in my rear bedroom. He knew who I was and what I was doing but had studiously refrained from asking questions. His message came like a thunderbolt.

"You're wanted in Washington at once," he said.

"What's up?" I asked, scarcely able to control my voice.

"War with Japan."

"I can't believe it."

"It will break any time now."

"You're an optimistic devil," I said, hoping against hope for the prospect of home.

"When can you leave?"

"Today," I said, "but I'll never get passage to Hong Kong. The wealthy Chinese who are running away have the CNAC booked up for months."

"I'll see that you get transportation over the lines."

"How about my boss, General—do you know his name?"

"Of course. I'll arrange your release."

A servant opened the door experimentally. "Another foreign gentleman," he announced. It was the doctor from the gunboat. He opened a black case and began to take out a number of bottles and instruments.

"Now what?" I asked.

"You can't land in Manila or the States without typhoid, smallpox, and cholera innoculation certificates."

"But I've already had them," I protested, "only thirty days ago."

"Chinese certificates," Doc said, laughing, "are no good. I'd take these a dozen times myself if it meant getting back home."

"I'm going back with you, Yardley," said the military commissioner.

"Taking Miss Wang with you?" I laughed.

He shook his head good-naturedly. Miss Wang was a singer at the Shanghai Sing-Song Theatre in Chungking, which had miraculously escaped destruction in the bombings, and she had been his favorite. "But I'll never forget your hospitality."

"You'll miss these yellow girls," I said.

"Yes, I suppose so."

"What are you going to do when you get lonesome for them?"

"I'll get me a pair of tinted glasses," he said.

Part Three

OTHER POKER GAMES

Part Three is purely expository. If the games in Part One and Part Two have been mastered, there will be no trouble in understanding the above games of poker.

I

Five-Card Stud with the Joker

The joker counts the same as in Jacks or Better with the Joker, page 127. Stay on the same cards as in Five-Card Stud, page 30, regardless of the joker.

II

Six-Card Stud

In this game you stay on any pair backed up because you have four more cards to make either three of a kind, two pair, or possibly a full house—this of course does not preclude the possibility of a straight, straight flush, or flush.

For example, suppose you have two deuces back to back and draw an eight. You now have 2 2 8 and have three more cards (not two as in five-card stud) to help the hand.

The rest of the staying requirements are the same as in Five-Card Stud, pages 40-41.

Six-Card Stud with the Joker

The joker counts the same as in Jacks or Better with the Joker, page 127. The staying requirements are the same as in six-card stud, regardless of the joker.

III

SEVEN-CARD STUD WITH VARIATIONS

1. *Betty Hutton*

Nines and fives are wild in Betty Hutton—either may represent any card. Five of a kind beats a straight flush. Five aces are the best hand. All the wild cards are underlined.

Stay on:

Any three wild cards:	5 9 5
Three aces	A A A
kings	K K K
queens	Q Q Q
jacks	J J J
Any two wild cards	5 9 x*
One wild card and one ace	5 A x
One wild card and one king	9 K x
Three-card straight flush in the same suit, jack or higher	Q J 10 ♠ ♠ ♠

Straights, flushes and full houses
    are not worth a call

* x equals any card.

2. *Doctor Pepper*

Tens, twos and fours are wild in Doctor Pepper and may represent any card. Five of a kind beats a straight flush. Five aces are the best hand. All the wild cards are underlined.

Stay on:

Any three wild cards   2 4 10

One wild card and two aces   2 A A

One wild card and two kings   4 K K

Any two wild cards   2 4 x*

Three-card straight flush in the
    same suit above a jack   Q J 10
    ♠ ♠ ♠

Straights, flushes and full
    houses are not worth a call

    * x equals any card.

3. Low

Turn to Seven-Card Stud, Hi-Lo, pages 100-107. You play seven-card stud Low the same as you do in seven-card stud Hi-Lo except that you do not go for a *High* hand. However, in seven-card stud Low, A 2 3 4 5 is the *lowest* hand in the deck, the same as five-card draw Low Ball. Of course this is a straight but straights are not counted as such.

Remember, in this game A 2 3 4 5 is the *lowest* hand; in Hi-Lo A 2 3 4 6 is the *lowest*.

4. High Hand with the Joker

The joker counts the same as in Jacks or Better with the Joker, page 127. The requirements to stay are the same as on page 82.

5. Low Hand with the Joker

The joker counts as an ace only in this game. The requirements to stay on the first three cards are the same as in Seven-Card Stud, Low, pages 100-107.

6. *Hi-Lo with the Joker*

The joker counts the same as in Jacks or Better with the Joker, page 127.

The requirements to stay on the first three cards are the same as in Seven-Card Stud, Hi-Lo, pages 100-107.

7. *Baseball*

In this game all the nines and treys are wild. Any player who draws a trey *face up* must either put up the amount of the pot or fold. If a player is dealt a four face up he may call for another card, which is dealt to him face down.

Actually, the requirements to stay are too severe to risk buying the pot unless the trey makes you five queens, five kings or five aces. If you are playing a social game with pennies, stay. But if you are watching the pennies, fold before you get involved. If other players insist on playing this game, except for a round or so, don't put your feet under the table.

8. *Football*

The game is the same as Baseball except that sixes and fours are wild. A four in Football takes the place of the trey in Baseball. If a player is dealt a deuce face up he is entitled to another card face down —in other words the deuce in Football takes the place of the four in Baseball.

9. *Low Spade-High Hand*

In this game the player holding the *lowest spade face down* wins one-half of the pot, and the player holding the *highest* hand wins the other half. Of course, a player may win the entire pot by holding the low spade and the high hand.

Stay for low spade if you hold the five, four, trey or deuce of spades *face down*. If you Hold the deuce of spades face down, you may safely raise every pot.

For high, play the same as you would in seven-card stud—high.

This game, if possible, should be avoided because the element of chance is too great.

10. *Low Hole Card Wild*

Wild cards are the *lowest* card or cards held in your hand face down, that is, the *lowest* you hold in the first, second and seventh cards which are all down-cards. For example, suppose the first two cards (face down) are a trey and a seven, and the last (down card) is a deuce. Then all the deuces in your hand are wild, whether face up or face down. Also, suppose the first two cards are a pair of fives and the last card a trey. Then all the treys, face up and face down, are wild. Further, suppose the first two down cards are kings, and the last an ace. Then all the aces in your hand are wild.

It will be readily seen that if the first and second cards pair (jacks, for instance) it may look as if you have a good start because both these cards are wild, but if the last card is *higher* than jacks—a queen, for instance—the value of your hand may be materially lessened because only the queens will be wild.

This game should be avoided because of the element of chance.

IV

FIVE-CARD DRAW WITH VARIATIONS

1. *Jacks or Better with the Joker*

In this game the joker may represent only the ace or any card to fill in either a straight or a flush. For example, joker ace equals two aces. Joker king would represent only one king and the beginning of a possible straight or flush. Joker 4 5 6 7 is a straight, and joker 7 J K A is a flush.

♣ ♣ ♣ ♣

The staying requirements are the same as in Five-Card Draw, Jacks or Better; that is, you open on kings or better.

2. *Queens or Better with or without the Joker*

The joker counts the same as in Jacks or Better with the Joker, page 127. Stay on kings or better.

3. *Kings or Better with or without the Joker*

The joker counts the same as in Jacks or Better with the Joker. Stay on kings or better.

4. *Aces or Better with or without the Joker*

The joker counts the same as in Jacks or Better with the Joker. Stay on aces or better.

5. *Anything Opens with or without the Joker*
also
Any Pair Opens with or without the Joker

The joker again counts the same as in Jacks or Better with the Joker.

Since any five cards may open or any small pair, more players naturally stay in this game and draw cards to small pairs, two face cards, a three-card flush or straight; in fact, anything after the pot is opened. But just because the pot may be opened on anything or any small pair is no excuse for the careful player to open or stay on weak hands. You should open or stay on the same requirements as in Five-Card Draw—that is, kings or better. To play on small pairs, two face cards or three-card straights and flushes is simply throwing away your money.

You should study Five-Card Draw, Jacks or Better, beginning on page 3 before playing this game.

6. *Low Ball with the Joker*

The requirements to stay are the same as in Five-Card Draw, Low Ball, pages 71-75, regardless of the joker.

In this game the joker counts the same as an ace only.

7. *Spit-in-the-Ocean*

This game is a variant of deuces wild, five-card draw, except that only four cards are dealt to the players. A fifth card is dealt face up in the center of the table and is wild, which gives everyone a wild card. The other three cards of the same denomination are also wild.

The percentages in this game are about the same as in Five-Card Draw, Deuces Wild, page 51 except that spit-in-the-ocean has only four wild cards and deuces wild has four wild deuces and the joker.

More players will stay in this game than in deuces wild because everyone has a wild card in the center of the table to start with. But my advice to you is: under no circumstances be influenced to stay because of this. Refer to Five-Card Draw, Deuces Wild, and the list of hands you should hold, page 51, before staying.

Now and then you will run into a poker game not treated in this book, but if you have mastered the foregoing you will be able to play the new game skillfully by comparing it to one of those I have covered.